A READING FOR HR PROFESSIONALS

A READING FOR HR PROFESSIONALS

Dr. H.L. Kaila

Publications

KALPAZ PUBLICATIONS

DELHI - 110 052

A Reading for HR Professionals

Rs. 650

ISBN : 81-7835-395-4

Published in 2005 in India by
Kalpaz Publications,
C-30, Satyawati Nagar,
Delhi-110 052
Email : kalpaz@hotmail.com

Lasertype Setting by: Tact Computer Graphics, Delhi
Printed at: Mehra Offset Press, Delhi

This book is dedicated to all those human resource professionals and learners of the world who make difference in the quality of life of people with their attitudes, behaviours and art of HRD for achieving business goals.

Contents

Preface 9

Acknowledgements 15

1. Recent HR Researches 17
2. The Psychological Constructs of Managers 109
3. Stresses, Health Problems, and Coping Mechanisms of HR Managers 129
4. The Current HR Scenario 141
5. The New Human Resources Professional 157
6. Women Managers 177

Bibliography 199

Index *209d*

Preface

Some of the major areas that HR research has focused upon are: the emerging challenges of the human resources professional, business relationships and environment, HR strategies, new initiatives, leadership, policies, managing change, safety and health care services. The facts derived from the HR researches indicate that:

- The new roles of the HR manager are emerging which are mainly decisional, interpersonal, and informational.
- HR professionals have gained focus and prominence in business decisions.
- Managing a group of heterogeneous people is a formidable task to modern managers.
- The communication sensitivity is something that the HR manager must possess.
- The greatest challenge facing HR managers is to find ways of empowering the employees.
- The HR managers have to be sensitive towards human values and needs of employees, and the concerns of the organization.
- The human resource professionals have crucial role to play in managing change in the organization.
- The customer relationship management strategy is a new area towards which the HR professionals are contributing.
- The major concern of HRD is achieving and maintaining a satisfied workforce.
- The HR managers need to be knowledgeable about business trends and issues.

- A goal of HR specialists is to empower employees to manage their own stresses and achieve better health.
- HR managers must be in regular touch with the key line managers and staff.
- They need to be innovative towards improving organizational performance.
- They need to develop systems such as objective performance feedback, career planning and development, and internal networking.
- Without the integrated human resource policies and strategies, organizations are less likely to survive.
- The human resource managers play an increasingly significant role, as the organizations take diversity initiatives.
- The ultimate goal of HR managers is to achieve the learning and self-sustaining organization.
- The proactive and business oriented human resource managers have to become the catalysts of change.

The current HR scenario features the following:

- Human Resource Management has come a long way and the companies are stressing the importance of people.
- Management of human resource is today vital to every company and industry.
- The human resource activities have widened its scope including a range of crucial issues right from recruitment to the international human resource management covering corporate training, improvement management, communications, welfare, safety and health.
- The HR professional champions the identification and implementation of the organizational mission, vision, values, goals, and action plans.
- Creating a committed workforce is the main function of the HR professional in any organization today.
- Though there are certain common roles and responsibilities of the HR personnel, different organizations employ HR

Managers for different nature of job as per needs of the organization.

The characteristics of the new human resource professional are:

- The most important quality of a HR manager is to deal successfully with people.
- The HR professionals have moved up to the higher echelons in the organizations.
- They need business perspective orientations as the HRD policies are being integrated into the overall policies of the organization.
- The challenge of HR department is to perform towards the fullest growth and utilization of their human resources for the development of the organization.
- The female managers perceive themselves established in their organization.
- The HR managers face a variety of stresses such as meeting deadlines, making decisions, multi-tasking, selecting and retaining competent people, long hours of work, coordination of resources, internal politics and being cost-effective.
- The stresses experienced by HR personnel are of varied nature. They have to prepare themselves as per needs of the organizational circumstances.
- The occupational psychosomatic health problems such as acidity, headache, tiredness, back pain, aches in the neck, hypertension and blood pressure problems are being faced by the HR manager.
- The health maintenance of HR managers is significant to the organizational performance, growth, and development. The organizations must take care of the managerial well being.
- They have developed personal management skills and strategies to keep themselves fit. Some of these are: relaxation, reading, meditation, talking with colleagues, yoga, attending

training courses, time management, team work, exercise, and prioritizing work. The managers are trying hard to equip themselves to combat occupational stresses.

The HR field is under transition due to changes in the business scenario in the globalising society. An international HR professional is developing. The organizations expect the HR professionals to equip themselves in order to serve the cause of human resource development towards achieving business goals. The stresses of the HR personnel are too many. Though they are evolving their coping strengths, the organizations need to ensure the physical, mental and social well being of HR managers so that they can work towards the development of a better business environment and the healthy organizations.

This book *A reading for HR professionals* has been presented as a resource material in order to enhance the knowledge of HR managers through the annotated research abstracts and the experiences of managers from several companies provided inside this presentation.

This work, organized in six chapters, reflects upon the emerging functions of HR managers, and their perceptions on the current HRD scenario. This is a careful selection, compilation and comprehensive review of researches carried out by Indian and foreign researchers that would help the HR professionals understand and reexamine objectively as to what are the human resource issues, and how they are being tackled in organizations. This book would also help understand the stresses and health problems of HR managers, and importantly how do they cope with the challenges of human resource capital.

This volume has brought out researches with all those issues that attracted the attention of industry, on the issue of human resource management. The literature review of studies during, the past 10 years indicates the research trends on HR issues.

This presentation is original, and aims at developing insights for better human resource management. The aim of this book is to present the researched knowledge on crucial HR by issues. The students of Management, Commerce, OB, HR, and the allied fields at the universities, colleges, and professional institutions shall find the book a useful text. All the young as well as experienced managers shall benefit and find it meaningful for their own and organization's better growth. This publication provides an educator for one and all those who happen to be a learning manager.

Dr. H.L. Kaila

Acknowledgements

I would like to express my sincere gratitude to the following professionals for their informal and formal contributions:

- Prof. Rupa Shah: Vice Chancellor - SNDT Women's University;
- Dr. Usha Nayar: Deputy Director, TISS;
- Sh. Thomas Mathew; Sr. Vice President, Reliance Group;
- Dr. A Gangopadyay-Prof. PMIR, TISS;
- Dr. A. Gangopadyay – Prof. PMIR, TISS;
- Sh. Thomas Mathew: Sr. Vice President, Reliance Group;
- Dr. S.V. Surnis, Head –Commerce Dept. Chetana College, Mumbai;
- Dr. Satish Pai: Chief – Management Development, BSES;
- Dr. Reeta Sonawat: Reader, Human Development;
- Dr. A.G. Bhalwankar: Director, BCUD, SNDT Women's University;
- Prof. Jitendra Mohan: Dept. of Psychology, Punjab University;
- Dr. K.B. Kushal: Regional Director – D.A.V. Schools;
- Dr. Henal Shah: Secretary – Bombay Psychiatrist Association;
- Dr. Manisha Sen: Prof. of Psychology; Mumbai University;
- Sh. Asis Chakarborty: Director – Industrial Psychology, CLI;
- Dr. Harish Shetty: Social Psychiatrist;
- Dr. Anjali Chhabria: Child Psychiatrist;
- Fr. Berkie, Director, St. Xavier Institute of Counseling;
- Dr. Harshida Pandit: Senior Psychologist;

- Mrs. Bharti Gandhi: Director - Youngbuzz;
- Mrs. Meera Bakshi: Ex-Educational Advisor, Ambani Schools;
- Dr. Parul Rishi, Lecturer – PM & OB, IIFM, Bhopal;
- Prof. Deepak K. Behera, Sambalpur University, Orissa.

Dr. H.L. Kaila

1

Recent HR Researches

This section has brought out the facts based on researches carried out by Indian and foreign researchers that would help the HR professionals understand and reexamine objectively as to what are the human resource issues, and how they are being tackled in organizations. This volume has brought out researches with all those issues that attracted the attention of industry, media, and the government on the issue of human resource management.

This literature review of past 10 years explains the phenomenon of HR management in its factual way. This analysis indicates the research trends and the shift that took place and the interest of researchers on HR issues as the decades passed. Each of the research studies has been annotated in this section, the description of which provides scientific information to HR professionals to broaden their understanding on the whole gamut of issues involved in HR development and management.

The New Role of the Human Resources Professional

Some industry commentators call the Human Resources function the last bastion of bureaucracy. Traditionally, the role of the Human Resource professional in many organizations has been to serve as the systematizing, policing arm of executive management. In this role, the HR professional served executive agendas well, but was frequently viewed as a roadblock by the rest of the organization. Much of the HR role is transforming itself.

The role of the HR manager must parallel the needs of his changing organization. Successful organizations are becoming more adaptable, resilient, quick to change direction, and customer-centred. Within this environment, the HR professional, who is considered necessary by line managers, is a strategic partner, an employee sponsor or advocate, and a change mentor.

In today's organizations, to guarantee their viability and ability to contribute, HR managers need to think of themselves as strategic partners. In this role, the HR person contributes to the development of and the accomplishment of the organization-wide business plan and objectives. The HR business objectives are established to support the attainment of the overall plan and objectives. The tactical HR representative is deeply knowledgeable about the design of work systems in which people succeed and contribute. This strategic partnership impacts HR services such as the design of work positions; hiring; reward, recognition, and strategic pay; performance development and appraisal systems; career and succession planning; and employee development.

As an employee sponsor or advocate, the HR manager plays an integral role in organizational success via his knowledge about and advocacy of people. This advocacy includes expertise in how to create a work environment in which people will choose to be motivated, contributing, and happy. Fostering effective methods of goal setting, communication, and empowerment through responsibility build employee ownership of the enterprise. The HR professional helps establish the organizational culture and climate in which people have the competency, concern, and commitment to serve customers well. In this role, the HR manager provides employee development opportunities, employee assistance programs, gain sharing and profit-sharing strategies, organization development interventions, due process approaches to problem solving, and regularly scheduled communication opportunities.

The constant evaluation of the effectiveness of the organization results in the need for the HR professional to frequently champion change. Both knowledge about and the ability to execute successful change strategies make the HR professional exceptionally valued. Knowing how to link change to the strategic needs of the organization will minimize employee dissatisfaction and resistance to change. The HR professional contributes to the organization by constantly assessing the effectiveness of the HR function. He also sponsors change in other departments and in work practices. To promote the overall success of his organization, he champions the identification of the organizational mission, vision, values, goals, and action plans. Finally, he helps determine the measures that will tell his organization how well it is succeeding in all of this (Susan M. Heathfield, 2001).

HR Professionals Gain Credibility with New Designation

In the corporate culture of twenty or thirty years ago, most people worked for one employer for their whole career. They made a living wage, with expected increases based on both promotion and seniority, and retired with a set pension and a gold watch. Employee relations was handled by the personnel department, who managed some of the hiring and benefits as well as any training that the company might find necessary from time to time. The people who staffed and ran these departments had no specific training, and sometimes no related skills.

"People who had a warm personality and a nice handshake were put off into the personnel department," says Dr. Craig Pinder, of the more than 2,000 member strong B. C. Human Resource Management Association. "Sometimes that department ended up with the company's deadwood."

In today's business world, the human resource department has to deal with ongoing issues that span the range of recruitment, hiring, training, employee relations, systems analysis and management. Jobs are no longer for life; as the economy shifts from a resource base to being service and information technology industry driven, people are changing companies and even career four and five times in a lifetime. The role of the human resource professional within a company has gained focus and importance as companies strive to systemize the management of human resources.

"The role of the human resource practitioner today is to enable the organization to be successful through good people practices," explains BCIT's head of Human Resource Management program Eileen Stewart.

These 'good people practices' extend well beyond hiring. In fact, most human resource professionals do not actually hire staff. They may set out strategies and implement plans that allow a company to attract the right people, they may act as researchers and pre - screeners, but they leave the hiring to the line managers - the people for whom the new staff will be working. Human resource managers tend to focus their energies on developing and administering the programs that effect all of the company's employees, like pension plans, workplace health programs, employee and labour relations and compensation programs. In a climate that includes wrongful dismissal suits, sexual harassment issues and an ongoing turnover of staff, they can act as a guide that will give the company a healthy direction and relationship with its employees. They need to know the systems that are necessary to manage staff and analyze present and future needs for a company, and the laws and regulations that both employers and employees must abide by. More than that, they need to fully understand their company's business and their industry.

"You have to understand the corporate culture" says George Muenz, human resources manager for Net Nation Communications, a Vancouver e-commerce and internet provider, who sees this as particularly true in the fast changing high tech field. "For instance, high tech workers are exempt from some standard labour practice codes. They live in a different world than most industries. The policies we develop - and the way they're implemented - have to reflect that."

High tech has been a great example of an industry that needs good human resource managers. It's relatively new, the companies are generally small to medium sized, and their need for people has often been large and immediate. The competition for really good people is still intense, a human resource manager may be asked to research what a young company will have to pay, including possible stock options, bonuses and relocation costs. They may direct as to where the hiring company should look, and how to best attracts the right people. Finally, they may provide training programs and strategies for in - house development to allow the company to build a stable workforce.

On the other side of the human resource coin, many larger companies, particularly those in resource-based industries, as well as many of those upstart high technology's, are downsizing. Human resource managers are involved in defining which positions might be cut, in developing acceptable severance packages, and in 'outplacement' services - counseling and training that make it easier for the former employee to re-enter the work force (and less likely that they will leave acrimoniously).

In the middle, HR managers are involved in labour negotiations and salary arbitration's, as well as helping to develop ongoing staff-management communication strategies and monitor both the need for, and effectiveness of, professional development and training programs. As the awareness that happy and healthy employees are a vital part of successful business grows, so does the role for these qualified professionals. While many are graduates of university business administration courses and technical institute diploma programs, the profession is currently striving to make itself more accountable. Joan Harrison, who acts as director of professional designation for the BCHRMA, says the HRMA's national Certified Human Resources Professional (CHRP) designation program is geared to bring stronger credibility to human resource professionals in Canada.

"The CHRP designation has been awarded to applicants on the basis of a combination of education and experience," notes Harrison, "We're now less than a year away from standardized exams across the country - very similar to those undertaken by chartered accountants."

While the new national designation may cast more light on this growing profession, companies in every avenue of business have come to recognize the value of trained professionals in managing what many see as their single most valuable asset.

"The ability to move through changing times, and to leverage that change in a positive way, is the reason that human resource people now report directly to the president of many companies," says Harrison. And she believes the new national designation will be not only looked upon favorably but also demanded by industry.

"Within two years, all the generalists will need the designation to practice in the [human resources] field," she predicts. "It's becoming the symbol of the industry." In B. C., where few large companies base their head offices and the economy overall has dictated less activity in every area of business, human resource professionals may find full time work sometimes difficult to find, but opportunities for employment don't stop there. Many small and mid sized companies are looking for outside help when it comes to human resource problems and projects, and are hiring HR professionals in a consulting or contractual role.

"If you're looking for a traditional 9 to 5 job in the human resource department of a big corporation, you might be disappointed," says BCIT's HRM program head Eileen Stewart, "But the opportunity to work on individual projects and contracts is almost unlimited."

As people and their skills become an ever more valuable part of every business, the need for human resource professionals can only grow (Malmgren, J.K. 2001).

Managers Leadership

Manager roles are mainly decisional, interpersonal, and informational for effective role-playing. It is expected that they possess technical human and conceptual skills.

Many management tools are drawn from the research done in various disciplines. All these aspects find coverage in this text.

This book (S. Shiva Ramu, 2000) attempts to map the development of various management tools and techniques during the 20th century. It is a modest attempt at being comprehensive but it is not exhaustive. It starts with scientific management propagated at the beginning of the century. The nature of facts and fashions are described with some hero leader's biographies.

The author has recognized the complexity and dynamics of environmental changes during the end of the century. These have been addressed in different ways.

The chapter selected starts with differences between the characteristics of a manager and a leader and how to achieve managerial effectiveness. Different authors either use different dimensions or different styles of management to identify an effective manager style.

Management Development—Purpose, Process and Prerequisite

This book (Jean Woodall and Diana Winstanley, 2000) provides an overview of our knowledge of what is happening in management development in theory, research, and practice. This text is intended to take a more critical approach than many standard textbooks on management development in identifying the themes and contradictions. The focus is on the strategic organization level and the role of management development in contributing to organizational to aims as well as individual objectives. It provides a general overview of manager's learning and cautioned against as uncritical acceptance of prevailing fashion. In particular, the self-sustaining learning organization may be the espoused goal of many managers. Indeed in a world of growing employment insecurity where self-development and unemployment are likely experiences for most managers may not just want to learn from the work-related learning opportunity, but may also value the social learning and formal credentials that come with off-the-job development and management education.

Introduction of Technical Change in the Organization

The book (Jean Woodall and Diana Winstanley, 2000) contained a collection of well-researched case studies and condensed insights generated out of in-depth research. Chapter 6 essentially focused on the introduction of technical change in the organization, employee involvement thereafter (team working, quality circles, joint consultation and collective bargaining with trade unions) as well as the introduction of technical change in a non-union environment and the importance of management style in introducing technical change, i.e., paternalistic versus interactive communication. The degree of involvement of the HR specialist depends to a large extent on the nature and role of the HR function within any particular organization. When there has been informal resistance from employees over IT implementation it unfortunately tends to be viewed as a workforce systems problem and the responsibility of line management rather than HR. The results of the Workplace Employee Relations Survey indicate that generally there is a low level of involvement of human resource or personnel a manager in technical change. Though it is argued that this is likely to result where the investment in information technology is regarded as routine since human resource specialists have no 'natural' involvement in operating decisions and change initiatives thereafter.

The Personnel Function, HR and the Future

For many employees the suspicion remains that HR is another device, the latest fad to provide a moral cloak of respectability concealing the true purpose of business i.e., to reduce costs and make a fast buck. However, there should be little doubt that a HR manager or professional within an organization plays a crucial role. While team building camps and the like are enjoyable learning experiences they do not necessarily translate to commitment. The HR function is therefore to persuade managers to drop the traditional approaches to people and work towards a position of mutuality and trust. The HR manager must guard against a dependence on fads, the main question being whether the suggested new technique is simply a repackaging of an old one or whether it provides a change of real substance. Many organizations look at the cost of recruitment, training etc. and come to the decision that they can save by getting someone outside the organization to contract for the task however the HR manager will be working on people management strategies that are central to the organization and cannot be out-sourced. Finally HR managers should beware of fashionable HR speak, as it will quickly lead to discredit (Braham, J. 1994).

Devising Human Resource Development Strategies

No longer is human resource management the sole province of a personnel specialist; it is the priority of every manager who has line responsibility for staff. Moreover without integrated human resource policies and strategies, organizations are less likely to survive today. A survey of ninety Irish high technology companies revealed that 95 per cent of companies had an established HRD function; 81 per cent had a written HRD policy statement. In addition to which it was found that the individuals identified as being responsible for implementing the HRD plan varied widely: 41 per cent saw it as the sole responsibility of the HRD manager, 35 per cent indicated that it was the responsibility of the HRD specialist and the line manager, 8 per cent the line manager only and 16 per cent the human resource manager. Some organizations have impressive training plans, which result in little development of the staff while others may have little in the way of elaborate HRD plans and experience development at all levels. Essentially what creates the difference between them is the identification of the skill performance gap by able HR professionals who then capitalize on internal forces for change and minimize the restraining forces from both within and outside the organization creating successful, innovative organizations (Thomson, R. and Mabey, C. 1994).

Role of HR in Acquisitions

Acquisition talks are at an advanced stage between Gentech and HCC, two software giants when the HRD Head of Gentech demands a place at the negotiations. She is concerned about the lack of attention to people issues which can ruin the perfect fit between companies—apart from incompatible cultures, issues like loss of key talent and clash of management styles will pop up. HCC's CEO too is concerned with HR implications of the merger as employees have begun to feel that they will be bossed over. HRD Head of Gentech joins the negotiations although the HCC team is given no intimation. Case analysis was provided by experts who concur that 47 per cent of managers leave within 1 year as one week after a merger announcement, competitors and head hunters move in on the best talent hence one cannot 000and should not ignore human resource issues in any merger and acquisitions discussion. Furthermore it must be understood that a distinction exists between the process of acquisition and the process of making it work. The role of HR should therefore be considered as early as possible in acquisitions and the HR heads of both companies should have had a place at the talks (Krishnan, R. 2002).

Managerial Leadership Skills

The manager needs to demonstrate three kinds of technical competence to be accepted as a leader-, that which relates to the product and technology of the enterprise, that which has to do with his technical competence in his specialty as befitting his level in the managerial hierarchy and that involved in his practice of the act of management. The lower the rank of the manager, the less he would be expected to know about the minute technical details of the product or its production. The higher his rank, the more he would be expected to know about the less tangible aspects of the operation, such as long range planning, financial company growth, or judging the quality of an intended acquisition. The management jobs at the lower levels of the organization pyramid are, in general, constrained by the technology of the organization; their scope is narrow and they deal in the hard realities of work pushing and production schedules. Conversely, the higher the management job, the less sharply defined conditions become and the greater the need for play of the imagination in the development of innovative solutions to organizational problems.

The manager should strive to achieve proficiency in these technical areas. He should have a reasonably sound grip of the technical process of the company and the specialty in which he is working. He should be seen to keep abreast of advances in his technical field. For example a financial officer should keep up with changes in the federal tax laws, understand their implication and know-how to benefit his company by applying this knowledge. Or a vice-president for marketing should know and be able to use new concepts in identifying special segments of his company's market.

In the same fashion, the manager should know the technical aspects of management practice appropriate to his status. For example, if he has a group of subordinate managers reporting to him, he should know how to run a meeting efficiently. He should know the theory and practice of non-directive counseling and how to build teamwork in his group. He should be able to perform well in planning and budgeting as well as in many other areas that lie somewhere between science and art.

Competence in administrative process supports the manager in the performance in his roles as problem solver, communicator, and integrator. Competence in dealing with administrative matters enables him to use the system to help him achieve his goals. He can be backing it.

Technological change, with its increasing complexity, has brought the need to weld the efforts of many different kinds of specialists to accomplish the goals of the enterprise. Seldom does one have the technical competence to comprehend, let alone direct, the many activities that must be integrated to achieve success in today's enterprise. There must be genuine cooperative effort, based on mutual trust and respect among people. Effective collabouration results from participative style of management symbolizing the synergism of true cooperation. Research and behavioural science clearly shows that under proper management human potential may be realized in a way beneficial to the individual and to his organization.

As the pace of scientific discovery and its consequent technology accelerate, management will have to concern itself more and more with overcoming the communication barriers at the transactional interfaces between men of specialized educational backgrounds. This factor, plus growing social pressure for recognition of the individual and the movement toward group-centred-management, demands a high level of interpersonal competence in its manager. If a man has this kind of interpersonal competence, it can be seen in the way he isolates the important problems that face his group and the organization. It can be seen in the supportive way in which he deals with this people in solving these problems and in seeking acceptance of the solution by the group once individual differences have been resolved.

Under participative group-centred-leadership, the manager's leadership is authorized more by his technical and inter-personal competence than by the power of his formal position. He is required to accept and fulfill his responsibilities through adaptive responses to the reality of human behaviour. Social forces, too, are changing the values that surround the individual and the way in which he is perceived in our society. The wide diffusion of education has lead to a sharper and more compassionate view of the individual. His personal values must respect the worth and the dignity of the individual and his management styles must support human growth. In a climate of openness and trust, the manager can choose the most advantageous way of getting the specific task done in the full knowledge that his people will follow his leadership.

To be successful, the manager must show ability as a leader particularly in his roles as innovator, organization designer, supporter, mentor, and advocate. From the manager's point of view the important result of each cycle of equilibrium seeking between growth seeking entities like organization, group and individual should be the achievement of some kind of success–in production, design, improved methods, or other desirable ends. The pursuit of a desirable end, or goal implies overcoming obstacles or recovering an acceptable level of performance, in one way or another. The manager's influence as a change agent directly affects both the rate and quality of the behavioural changes needed to accelerate the achievement of organizational group and individual goals.

The manager's responsibility as coach and counselor requires him to make available education and training in technical and interpersonal competence in his group. He should see that advances in technical knowledge are made available to his group. He should act as a model of healthy interpersonal behaviour and support the development of interpersonal competence through coaching and counseling, through effective group processes and through the help of training when required.

The manager's basic roles demand facility in the use of language, both oral and written as his successful performance depends on the generation of sound ideas and the transfer of these ideas to others. Language affects both. Ideas are inherent in words.

Those who command many words command many ideas, fluency in the use of words underscores facility in developing ideas. Similarly, fluency in the use of language facilitates the transfer of ideas to others. Much of the manager's time involves communicating with others: issuing requests and instructions, giving information, asking questions, writing memos and letters and translating the special language of one technical group to another.

Fluency alone is not enough. In addition, those adroit in using language for its intended purpose deliberately adapt the level of their audience.

An organization functions by integrating the efforts of individuals, groups and departments; this process involves transactions between people at all levels. The manager's job is particularly sensitive here, since he represents the efforts of his group, department, or even larger unit. He practices advocacy, willy-nilly, in the transactions across organizational interfaces.

His working life revolves around a continuing series of negotiations with his fellow managers, his superiors, and his subordinates. He also frequently engages in transactions with the special community that makes up the enterprise's environment. His aim is to ensure fair distribution of workload, to decide on schedules, goals, and action plans and in all these negotiations to perform ably as an advocate for his ideas, his group, and his organization. In these efforts, his negotiating skill supports his managerial roles of advocate and integrator.

The quality of his advocacy is a highly visible aspect of his performance. He gains the respect of his group by being perceived as able to influence the management hierarchy above him in ways beneficial to the group. He gains respect in the organization by influencing his peer and subordinate managers in ways perceived as beneficial by management. His persuasiveness, his technical, administrative and social competence, and his ability to lead his group through pitfalls to successful accomplishment are observable through the quality of his advocacy. Competence in advocacy augurs well for success at higher management levels.

The role of top manager is to coordinate the subsystems within the company with super ordinate systems outside. Corporate performance in the ultimate analysis is the result of a company interacting with its environment rather than the result of factors wholly within the company itself. Super ordinate systems such as political, social, economic, society, government and several others impinge on corporate life very intimately and it is the function of a good organization to achieve a symbiosis, i.e., mutually beneficial living together of two dissimilar organisms with a variety of external systems. The systems approach implies a concept of wholeness where the whole is invariably greater than the sum total of individual parts. Viewed thus, the role of a manager running, as ongoing business enterprise is to constantly find ways and means of relating his activities to the wider framework of which his business is a part.

The success of the manager is measured in terms of organizational results in terms of output and services and it demands on the manager—maturity, adaptability, practical insights combined with the ability to take a fresh view of the situation (Satish Pai, S Ravishankar et al, 1999).

Challenges Faced by H.R. Managers

HR managers are facing many challenges these days. Some of them are listed down here.

Enlarging the scope on Personnel Management: The concept of personnel management has undergone tremendous changes in the recent times. In the past, scope was confined to "Health and Happiness" by organizing parties and picnics. Today the scope is enlarged to include every activity of the organization which has a human dimension, i.e., recruitment, selection, job design, job analysis, motivation, morale, human development, empowerment of employees etc. in the past manpower was considered as one of the many resources. Today manpower is the most important of all resources.

Experience of the current period of industrialization focus our attention to knowledge and skill of employees, the success and survival of an enterprise depend not on the number of employees or extent of capital it owns nor the present market standing. It depends mainly on the knowledge and skill of its people. Hence the focus is on persons and their development.

Globalization of economy and liberalization of trade has enlarged the scope and scale of operations of organizations. Emergence of multinational corporations (MNC) was the result. Of late MNCs have given way to transnational corporations (TNCs). In MNCs and TNCs the firms are widely dispersed all over the world. Employees of such organization come from different countries and nations having dissimilar culture, philosophy, and value systems. Managing a group of heterogeneous people throw greater challenges to modern managers.

Globalization of business is the modern trend focus on market economy dismantles the artificial trade barriers built up by nation, sooner than later. In globalization and liberalization of trade, working relationships between managers and employees, managers and suppliers, managers and customers etc. must undergo a sea of changes. International management has now emerged as a specialized field. In globalization "relationship network" and "relationship management" etc. have very important roles to play.

Management of human resources requires special skills. It is a complex job. This is because man himself is very complex.

Yet the manager must be able to predict employee's behaviour. While meeting the expectations of employees to motivate them, managers must also organization objectives are not sacrificed. When there is a clash of interest between individual and group interests the manager, more often than not, give emphasis to group interest against individual interest. Different persons are motivated by different means. This is because of their different personality, expectations, and perception. Success of manager depends on the unique way in which he is able to motivate each individual employee. Personnel management is not confined to personnel department. Wherever employees are engaged, personnel management exists. Thus we find all managers; irrespective of their specialization must be a master of human relations- skill. There are two types of managers- "task oriented" and "people oriented." In the long run, "people oriented" style is found successful. Modern management has developed a large number of techniques. In managing people the best technique is to love them. Where there is love there is sacrifice and concern in their well being. Where concern exists, mutual trust is developed. Trust and love increase morale, motivation, and efficiency. It also improves sense of belongingness and commitment, two factors, which promote empowerment.

Rapid industrialization has promoted large-scale production and bigger factories. This has also increased the number of employees. As their number increased the functions of personnel management got enlarged and complex. Widely dispersed production base and operating area further increased the scope of activities of personnel department. These activities are planning, coordination, direction, control and feedback, welfare steps, two-way communication, performance appraisals, objective assessment of task performance, rewards and punishment systems, career planning and promotions, retirement and replacement. Age-old obsession of centralization is found ineffective. Even the conventional concepts of decentralization is not found good enough to meet fast response time between action and reaction to meet intense market competitiveness of product and services. The need of the day is to prepare employees to become "self-directed" and "self-controlled."

Quality of employees: Quality of employees has also changed. They are now more and more educated and enlightened and economically stable even in developing countries. They are aware of their rights and privileges. Their expectation "on-the-job" and "off-the-job" are high. Managing them need better appreciation of their expectations and clear understanding of their psyche, feeling, attitude and sentiments. They are better organized and informed through public media, and unions. No more can they be taken for granted.

Sustainable competitive advantage: In globalization, success belongs to an organization whose product and services have competitive edge over the market in terms of price and quality. Continued innovation and improvement in product design, production methods, marketing techniques and customer interactions and earning their loyalty and goodwill sustain competitive advantage. All these are acquired, sustained and improved by actions of employees. In order to ensure that the employees are raised to the occasion they are to be highly motivated and enlightened, so that they become both innovative and creative. The real challenge to the modern personnel managers is how to bring them to that level of enlightenment.

Empowerment is the process of making ordinary employees to give extraordinary performance. As the time goes, competition is becoming very severe. Every organization is trying to build up enlightened group of employees who are innovative and creative. Every type of techniques is made to motivate them. The greatest challenge facing HR managers is to find ways and means of empowering their employees.

Mass movements like Industrial Revolution, Social Revolution has their impact on the ideological contents and policies of the government. Based on such peoples movement government has enacted a number of legislations. Such policies of government will have certain influence on the "personnel-policies" of the organization. In India we have legislations on "Factories Act," "Bonus Act", "Minimum Wages Act" etc. All these have profound influence on personnel management.

Business organization derives services from one section of the society and delivers services to another section of the society. But in the process the business firms earn the goodwill of the society and profit for their efforts. Thus, the very survival of organization depends on the goodwill and nourishment of the society. Thus, modern personnel manager will have "social responsibility" and "social responsiveness" as two most important functions to perform.

Disadvantaged sections of society have now become more and more articulate and put up their claim of selection and promotion. Public opinion and government support also go into their favour. This might be a challenge to merit in selection and promotion. Modern managers are exposed to such forces.

Manpower costs are to increase considerably which will cut down profit margin. Personnel managers will be under great strain to minimize manpower costs, at the same time acquire, and retain talented employees at attractive compensation. The only alternative is to derive maximum efficiency and productivity from employees. This requires higher skills in personnel management, which involve innovation in management so that interests of both the groups–employers and employees are attended to.

Challenges given above are some of the problems facing all managers and especially the personnel managers. As time goes, some of the problems may get solved; some may get acute: a few problems may arise. Public attitude towards work and working conditions changes from time to time. Similarly Government policies may vary from nation to nation and state to state. Practitioners and students of management must understand these problems so that they can be prepared to face them as they continue in their career to find suitable solutions, using their intelligence, innovative spirit and managerial skill (N.G. Nair and Latha Nair, 1999).

Communication Steps to be an Effective HR Manager

Communication is a very important aspect in which the HR Manager has to be well versed. Its only when his communication is effective will he be able to lead his team, take the right decisions and manage all the other functions that he is supposed to do.

Some things that a Manager should avoid while communicating:

Stop informing rather than persuading: With change being the norm rather than the exception in most organizations today, managers must stop thinking of communication as an exercise in information dissemination alone. The workforce today, particularly the younger potion, consistently requests more "why" and less "what."

Stop ignoring technological tools or using them incorrectly: Managers need to stop underutilizing the technology sitting at their fingertips. By not becoming adept at cyberspace navigation, one may run the risk of losing credibility with those more adroit than they lose. Even more importantly, productivity and efficiency may suffer in an era when speed is of the essence.

Stop undermanaging communication content and dissemination: The advent of more technological tools has created an abundance of unmanaged communication. No longer does information move up and down the ladder of the hierarchy, but, rather, moves here, there and everywhere. Access to information has opened up like floodgates and organizations need to develop ways to ensure the information is being utilized effectively. As the workforce becomes more involved in decision-making, it is critical that staff members have access to information formerly available only to managers. However, they must know how to access and use the information to make informed decisions.

Technology adds more options to the modes we can use to communicate and, therefore, presents great opportunity for organizations to go into information overload. As a leader, it is essential that you stop allowing this phenomenon to spread throughout your organization like an infectious disease.

Stop under-communicating the most important stuff: Research at Harvard University indicates that leaders communicate ten times less than they should when leading significant organizational change. Consequently, the rumor mill becomes overactive as staff members scramble to share what information they have heard. Too little shared information can be misleading, producing paranoia and undue stress, damaging productivity and morale. Under-communication can also mean too little listening. Managers sometimes forget that communication has two parts: sending and receiving.

Stop faking it: Unfortunately in our opinions, too many leaders pretend to listen to their staff. They ask for ideas and input, they don't follow up. The upshot is a disheartened team, feeling powerless and manipulated. Leaders may develop a great big credibility gap, losing their staff's trust.

Stop thinking locally: Leaders of today must consider the globe as their playing field. Your staff may now, or in the future, work worldwide, in person and/or online. Therefore, cross-cultural understanding becomes a prerequisite to effective cross-cultural communication. Thinking locally will not prepare you or your staff to meet this challenge, so stop limiting your scope.

Some things a manager must remember while communicating: Start thinking of yourself as a salesperson: Think of every communication you send as a presentation. It must be well oiled, polished, and add meaning to data. It must do more than inform; it must persuade, interpret, and educate. In the past, staff members, worked with groups of people for long periods of time and developed a shared body of knowledge and experiences. Now, with virtual teams becoming more the norm, staff must work quickly and be very good at what they do. Leaders have to communicate values and purpose, not just ideas to help staff–who may be spread all over the world–internalize the bigger meaning of their work.

Start setting communication standards: HR Managers should not let communication overload or dominate their organization. They should insist that work units employ rules concerning what gets communicated to whom, how often, and by whom. Once overload sets in, staff members begin to ignore a substantial amount of the communication they receive. Sometimes, managers forget that all parts of the organization may not be fully "wired" and, therefore, lose access to some communication. With flattening organization structures and more cross-functional team approaches, it is not always clear to whom staff members should go to get information. Therefore, guidelines as follows must be installed:

- What constitutes an urgent communication?
- Who needs copies and forwards of what kinds of information?
- What information should go to whom?
- Frequency with which files, electronic and otherwise, should be purged.
- Expected response time for each type of communication.
- Expected length of communication.
- Meeting norms.

Start getting buy-in through real participation and ownership: Communicating persuasively and listening actively are only part of the formula for effective communication. Interactions - live or via technology–is the critical variable in what we believe a manager must demonstrate. By ensuring staffs are actively involved in decisions that affect them, managers will maximize the brainpower running rampant in their organizations.

Start listening more: Another critical way to gain staff commitment and boost morale is to focus not only on sending messages, but also on receiving information. Many staff members don't believe their managers understand their concerns. As managers become more removed from the informal communication networks, or if they do not invite critical feedback, they will find the information that flows to them through formal channels is likely to be sanitized. No one really wants to be the bearer of bad news, unless the manager rewards the critic by listening, responding, and then taking action.

Start thinking globally: For those staff members who work across cultures, the manager has to make sure they have adequate training in cross-cultural communication. The manager's job is to ensure cultural sensitivity has been ingrained in the communication competencies of all staff working across borders (Louellen Essex and Mitchell Kusy, 2000).

HRM and its Strategies

According to Storey (1995), HRM is, 'a distinct approach to employment management which seeks to achieve competitive advantage through the strategic deployment of highly committed and capable, structural and personnel technique.'

HRM involves shift away from compliance with rules and procedures towards viewing personnel policy and practice as instruments for achieving strategic objectives.

Some HRM strategies: HRM is a whole bag of strategies ranging from selection and reward to appraisal and continuous improvement.

Communication: The conventional organization avoids communicating with the individual, either out of acceptance of the union agreement that direct communication subverts the collective or out of fear of reprisal. For HRM direct communication with employees is the most innocuous medium in HRM's repertoire, but also the most fundamental. It keeps the individual informed about a wide range of issues without the filtering medium of the trade union is of vital significance. Team briefing, house journals, employee reports, family day etc. have been used extensively as part of the effort to win the 'hearts and minds' of employees and promote their commitment to organizational objectives.

Participation: Used as synonym for employees' involvement, participation is for HRM a medium of directly involving employees on management terms, in managing specified activities where unions have no role.

The most participatory mechanism is the quality circle (QC). It is defined as, 'confirmation to customer expectation,' or 'more generally the pursuit of excellence.' QC may discuss the maintenance schedule for a machine, a safety problem or ways to cut down on input cost just as it may work to improve product or service quality. QC is very successful concept in Japan. QC fails because organizations were unable to cope with its consequences.

Total Quality Management (TQM) aims at getting workers to participate in the process of continuous improvement while leaving their managers alone. 3 features:

1st→top management is the engine of change.

2nd→innovation is considered to be essentially a managerial responsibility since it is the managers who have the authority to put things right.

3rd→continuous improvement requires cultural change in the organization.

Flexibility: In its quest to fully utilize the human resource, HRM seeks both numerical and functional flexibility.

Numerical flexibility is achieved by distinguishing between a privileged class of core workers with guaranteed employment and a subordinate class of peripheral or seasonal workers who are used to cope with shifts in demand.

Functional flexibility is a major objective for all core workers. Multi-skilling through skill development is at the centre of this process along with group work, job rotation, and job environment. The objective of seeking flexibility is undoubtedly the fuller utilization of the human resource.

Just-in-time (JIT): Above mentioned strategies were methods of achieving JIT the ultimate objective of the HRM. Its aim is to produce and deliver finished goods just in time to be sold sub-assemblies just in time to be assembled into finished goods, fabricated parts just in time to go into the sub-assemblies and purchased materials just in time to be transformed into fabricated parts.

JIT's answer to eliminate waste is to unproductive task by building production facilities around the product. This in HRM jargon is called cellular production an arrangement where every product becomes a relatively self-contained cell.

The method of just in case – organizations are so paranoid about the disruption of production schedules that they stockpile resources and build expensive buffers to meet any contingency. JIT in contrast is a pull system, which seeks to tailor production to real and not expected demand. It is about continuous improvement (E.A. Ramaswamy, 2000).

HR and its Role in Organization

World business scenario has recently been witnessing phenomenal changes in the facets and fronts of general management. Such changes are relatively more rapid in 1990s which represent the last decade of the last century before the next millennium. Sea changes have been taking place even in the Indian perspective. The trade globalization, disillusionment with state-owned enterprise, economic reforms packages, social emphasis of trade and industrial ecologization, public awareness and increasing competition from domestic as well as foreign big business–houses and so forth, have thrown serious challenges to Indian managers. Business managers should prepare themselves for the 21st century, in which their work ambit appears to be more enlarged.

In fact, general management is very exciting and dynamic discipline, but its excitement and dynamism mostly depends upon the intimate interaction between theory and practice. Today there is a need of the hour to charge depreciation on human body.

Human resource development / personnel / manpower management is concerned with obtaining and maintaining of a satisfactory and satisfied workforce, i.e., employees. It is a specialized branch of management concerned with 'man management.' The recruitment, placement, induction, orientation, training, promotion, motivation, performance appraisal, wages and salary, retirement, transfer, industrial relations, working conditions, trade unions, safety and welfare schemes of employees are included in personnel management. The object of personnel management is to create and promote team spirit among workers and managers (Singh H.K. and Singh Meera, 1998).

Successful Human Resource Attributes

(a) *Motivation:* the mainspring and driving force of initiatives. Attributes are:

- Dedication – the commitment that follows vision, empowers self and enables others.
- Credibility – defines self as a professional, take pride in the quality of work accomplished.
- Achiever – the internal drive to be up and doing, to get things done, energetic, competitive and on the fast track.
- Growth orientation – selects for talent, focuses on people's strengths, derives excitement and purpose from conceptualizing how they might foster growth.

(b) *Relationships:* interpersonal and coordinating strengths.

Attributes are:

- Developer – the desire to help other grow and develop as individuals, the capacity for taking satisfaction from each increment of growth of another person.
- Team – the capacity to get people to help each other use their goals.
- Arranger – the ability to coordinate people and resources for success, sophistication in understanding and working with organizational politics (Rosemary Thomson and Christopher Mabey, 1994).

New Mantras for 20th Century Management

Sharma has attempted to synthesize western management tools with eastern philosophy. He has suggested new concepts based on old concepts by modifying them a bit like 'old wine in new bottle', the concepts are:

OSHA model of human behaviour and action: three gunas–spiritual, human and animal, the guna theory is the basis for TQM (Total Quality of Mind). He also presents HQD (Human Quality Development) this is concerned with good governance and good management at the individual, organizational and societal level. These lead to the idea of

MIND – Manifestation of Infinity Diversity in Absolute.

SHE – Spiritualistic, Humanistic Existential.

SPOT – Similar to SWOT, but it concerns space and pace of opportunities and threats.

LIFE – Liberation from Exploitation.

MBA Model – Manas, Buddhi, and Ahankaar is suggested for decision making and interaction-cum-transaction analysis.

Motivation theory is modified to NEEDS – Necessities, Entitlements, Empowerment, Desires, and Self-realization. This leads to inspirational motivation or HOPE – Higher Order Purpose of Existence, which more than self-actualization.

VEDA – Vision, Enlightenment, Devotion, and Action.

SAR and RAS – Science, Art, and Religion – juice.

Above mentioned are some of the newer concepts growing and flowing in Indian industries. These are tools in the hands of HR managers, to better manage their human resources. Also greater importance has been given to individual and spiritual growth (S. Shiva Ramu, 2000).

Managing Change

In the industrial scenario, today change is taking place at a very fast pace and is causing a lot of adjustment problems and stress in the life of the employees. For example; changing working practices, installing a new computer system, attempting to shift the attitudes of the workforce, voluntary retirement, downsizing of employees' etc. Hence it is necessary for the organization to help their employees'.

The HRD plays a central role in managing organizational change in three ways:

1st – by responding to a succession of externally driven changes at an organizational level and to subsequent shifts in strategic direction, each of which has significant effects on development oriented practices in the workplace.

2nd – HRD can be and should have an influential role internally by developing and shaping the appropriate competencies and attitudes that will help the organization deliver its product and services.

3rd – HRD has a major role to play in the workforce, equipping them with the skills and know-how to cope with the change, are giving them a meaningful stake in the new regime.

The stimulus for change invariably comes from the external environment. The change affects a complex web of interrelated elements within an organization and trying to introduce change by addressing only one element in isolation will lead to a benefits that cannot be sustained in the long run. Each kind of change required slightly different HRD approaches to 'bed them in'.

The success of proposed change invariably relies on goodwill and commitment of those affected by them, which means giving staff access to decision-making and providing information (Rosemary Thomson and Christopher Mabey, 1994).

Causes of Work Related Accidents and Illness

The HR managers need to have knowledge about the work related accidents. The major causes of occupational accidents are:

- Tasks
- Working conditions
- Nature of the employee

Examples of causes related to the task and working conditions include poorly designed, inadequately repaired machines, lack of protective equipment, and the presence of dangerous chemicals or gases. Other working conditions that contribute to accidents including excessive working hours, leading to fatigue, noise, lack of proper lighting, boredom and horseplay and fighting. The National Institute for Occupational Safety and Health (NIOSH) is charged with finding out more about the causes of accidents and occupational health hazards.

There are data to indicate that some employees have more accidents than the average. Such a person is said to be an accident repeater. Employees who:

- are under 30 years of age,
- lack psychosomatic and perceptual skill,

- are impulsive and,
- are easily bored, are likely than others to have accidents.

Although some believe accidents processes can be measured by a set of attitude or motivational instruments, most experts who have examined the data carefully do not believe that attitudinal and motivational causes of accidents significantly influence accidents rates (John M. Ivancevich, 2001).

New Management Practices

Trends like globalization and technological innovation are changing the way firms are managed too the companies that have successfully responded to these challenges; new modes of organizing and managing have emerged, for example:

- The traditional pyramid-shaped organization is giving way to new organizational forms. At firms like AT&T the new way of organizing stresses cross-functional teams and boosting interdepartmental communications.
- Employees are being empowered to make more and more decisions.
- Flatter organizations are the norm instead of pyramid shaped organization with its seven to ten or more layers of management; flat organizations with just three or four levels will prevail.
- Work itself–on the factory floor, in the office even in the hotel – is increasingly organized around teams and processes rather than specialized functions.
- The bases of power are changing, i.e., positions; title and authority are no longer adequate tools for managers to rely on to get their jobs done. Instead success depends increasingly on tapping into sources of good ideas, on figuring whose collabourations is needed to act on those ideas and on working with both to produce results.
- Managers will not manage. Peter Drucker says that managers have to learn to manage in situations where they do not

command authcrity. The new manager thinks of himself or herself as a 'sponsor, team leader or internal consultant.'

- Managers today must build commitment (Gary Dessler, 1997).

Emerging HRM Practices

HRM in liberalized India presents an exciting opportunity for organizational level; the only remedy to cope with the fast changing global environment is to increase productivity, improve quality and deliver world class services. The onus of accomplishing these goals remains with the human resources in an organization.

Top Management: Perhaps the most formidable challenge of HRM is to change the key values, beliefs, and norms established by the top management.

Focus on Training: More or less, part of the responsibility of training employees with required skills rest with organizations and the HRM function in particular.

Pay and Compensations: The HRM function tends to play the role of aligning the reward system with the individual and group incentives, job redesign and individual and team participation.

Employee Relations: The unions are aware of their role in economic development and need for compromise and negotiation as opposed to a confrontational approach in problem solving.

Planning and Staffing: Formal and informal job descriptions were used for staffing purposes as well as for other HR activities.

Performance Appraisal: Self-appraisal, goals, objectives, and MBO were used, besides the traditional trait approach in assessing professional and managerial employees.

Compensation: For managerial levels in private organizations, promotion and pay increments were based on performance appraisal, while in the public sector both appraisal and seniority were considered.

The challenge of the HRM function will be to balance the negative impact of the much awaited exit policy possibilities with doses of motivation and productivity (Dwivedi, R.S. 1997).

Diagnostic Approach to Safety and Health: a Managers' Tool

The environmental factors important to health and safety are as follows:

- The most crucial factor is the nature of the task especially as it is affected by the technology and working conditions of the organizational environment.
- A second vital factor is employee's attitudes toward health and safety. Attitudes can vary from concern for safety and cooperation regarding safety programs to apathy. If employees are apathetic the best employee or safety program and the most stringent safety inspection by the HR will not improve conditions.
- The third factor affecting health and safety programs is economic conditions. Sometimes employer knowingly would choose to provide dangerous working conditions or would to provide reasonable safeguards for employees. But there is a lack of knowledge about the consequences of some dangerous working conditions and even when there is such knowledge economic conditions can prevent employers from doing all they might wish.
- A fourth factor is the unions. Many unions have been very concerned about the safety and health of their members and have pressured employers in collective bargaining for better proems.
- A fifth factor is management's goals. Some socially responsible managers and owners had active safety programs long before the lanes required them. They made safety and health an important strategic goal and implemented it with significant safety considerations designed into the enterprise's layout.
- A sixth factor affecting health and safety on the job is government. For years federal and state governments have attempted to legislate to improve occupational safety and health (John M. Ivancevich, 2001).

Problems of Job Stress and Burnout

Problems such as alcoholism and drug abuse sometimes result from stress, especially job stress. Here job related factors such as overwork relocation and problems with customers eventually put the person under such stress.

Environmental factors such as work schedule, pace of work, job security, route to and from rook and the member and nature of customers clients. The human consequences of job stress include anxiety, depression, anger, and various physical consequences, such as cardiovascular disease headaches and accidents.

Yet stress is not necessarily functional. Some people work wells only when under a little stress and find they are more productive as deadline approaches.

There are a number of things a person can do alternate stress, ranging from common sense remedies such as getting more sleep and eating better to more exotic remedies such as biofeedback and meditation. Finding a more suitable job, getting counseling and planning and organizing each activity are other sensible responses.

The organization and its HR specialists and supervisors can also play a role in identifying and reducing job stress. The HR specialist role including using attitude surveys to identify organizational sources of stress, refining selection and placement procedures to ensure effective person-job fit and providing career planning aimed at ensuring that the employee moves toward a job that makes sense in terms of her aptitudes (Gary Dessler, 1997).

Characteristics of HR in India

Human resources include both workers and managers. A study of the characteristics of these human resources in India forms a prerequisite to their effective management. The report of the National Commission on Labour (NCL) indicates the new book porch with the following background characteristics:

- There is substantial change in the social composition of workers. It is no longer limited to a particular caste or community. A mixed industrial force has emerged because of growing social mobility in the country.

- Traditional social banners are breaking down along Indian workers. The social distinction between a blue collar and a white collar is disappearing sharply.
- The distinction between manual and now manual rook force is also disappearing. This is true in view of the higher level of education and higher lunges of factory workers. The dignity of labour has increased and a greater sense of equality among workers has taken place.
- The Indian force is being characterized by charging sex composition. Educated women are coming forward to accept skilled and semi-skilled jobs in different industries.

Finally, there is a decline in the use of child labour although it still persists in several industries.

The attitudinal characteristics of Indian workers include:

- They have to make adequate adjustment with the nature of their job. They get conditioned to odd working situations involving obnoxious chemical, odours, temperature, noise, and humidity.
- They are politically conscious, articulate in their criticism of existing working order and sensitive to their conditions and hardships. They to the union to meet their exceptions and tend to choose the union which can deliver the 'economic' goods.
- They are not bothered whether their leader is an outsider or an insider. They tend to accept anyone who can fight for their cause and put across their grievances to the employer. They are also ready to pay for his services.
- Because of several employers based rummies they are sometimes equipped with negative attitude towards their employer. Disputes between employers and workers have been taking legalistic orientation of late mainly because of the emphasis on adjudication by industrial tribunals and courts.

Finally as the workers are not able to accomplish a standard they aspired they are more inclined to struggle for their right.

However it does not mean that they are blindfolded to public issues. Their attitude towards the Government is conditioned by its attitude towards them (Dwivedi, R.S. 1997).

Personnel and Human Resource Management

The Indian economy has become an integral part of the global economy. Globalization means facing the realities of competition, of producing goods and services of world standard quality. In such a fiercely competitive environment, with the liberalization and globalization of the economy, the management of the organization will have to initiate radical changes within the organization to enable it to compete effectively in a dynamic market. The managers of these organizations will have to become the catalysts of change.

The field of human resources is on the cutting edge of major social change. In today's highly complex environment, the programs developed, and the decisions made by human resource professionals profoundly impact the business firms profits and effectiveness (Sharma, A.M. 1994).

HR Managers Gear Up to Combat New Challenges

The career outlook for human resources professionals today, is stronger than ever. The external forces relating to corporate reorganizations, global competition, declining markets, changing work force, employee expectation represent long-term trends that have transformed the way organizations interact with employees. Human resource professionals are in a pivotal position in terms of these challenges.

Both historical and environmental forces created an urgent need for high quality human resource management in contemporary organizations. Today, many senior HR executives sit on the board of directors of corporation and represent the HR point of view. The organization-wide impact of human resource management, coupled with vital nature of the organizational processes involved, gives the human resource directors a great deal of influence in today's enterprise. A clear trend has emerged where higher proportions of HR directors become chief executives themselves.

What gives HR managers' sleepless nights? Expected to work as a negotiator, an implementers of the company's business objectives, play the perfect balancing between the employer and employees, there are many new challenges facing the HR managers in IT industry. It is believed that all these factors lead to hidden yet dominant fears, which can be dominant and affect their performance.

Though the HR issues have more or less remained the same, the managers are feeling the impact of challenges brought about by the revamping phase in IT industry. While earlier it was a matter of finding suitable candidates, now the performance factor has also come into picture. Besides this another constant of employees, which means continuously working towards creating new job opportunities and helping them grow in the organization. HR managers constantly worry about finding career enhancement to keep up morale of employees.

The retrenchment dilemma is one issue which HR managers would like to delete from their memory banks. Layoff of certain employees is a tough decision specially handling and dealing with complexities arising due to the kind of relationship you share with an employee also gives sleepless nights.

While tackling various issues, HR managers have to match up with the expectations of all concerned be it the boss, a subordinate, or even a colleague. Conflict can arise due to any small factor, whether it be welfare steps taken for an employee or going ahead with certain decisions, which may not be appreciated by many. Besides taking care of conflicts also which arise with line managers and other employees? HR managers have a lot of fire fighting in keeping the organization's image clean. Unless the expectations are handled properly by HR manager, it can create a lot of bad blood in the organization (Jorsotia Punita, 2002).

Employee Health and Safety

It has long been known that employee's health and safety are affected by the nature of the work they do and the environment they do it in. Health is a broader and somewhat more nebulous term than safety. A healthy person is one who is free from illness, injury, or mental or emotional problems that impairs normal human activities. Typically, safety concerns physical well being instead of mental or emotional well being.

Health promotion among managers should be an integral element of a business, company's strategy. The reason is that a healthy manager is a productive manager. Moreover, improvements in managers' health results in better work attitudes, higher morale and job satisfaction and reduced absenteeism and turnover, health promotion focuses on prevention rather than treatment or care. Hence, the health programs in an organization is normally planned around improvement and prevention of controllable risk factors such as smoking, obesity, stress, hypertension, low level of physical fitness which are responsible for many major diseases. The core health promotion activities to be included in a health care program may consist of exercise and physical fitness, smoking cessation, stress management, safety, and accident prevention, and maintaining health at the work place (Sharma, A.M. 1994).

Stress is a Major Concern of HR

Within the area of managers' welfare, space must be given to stress a major concern of those responsible for people at work; stress is becoming more common in organizations because of increasing job complexity and economic pressure on the individual. In the words of Cooper stress means: 'any force that places on the individual a psychological or physical factor beyond that individual's range of stability, producing a strain within the individual.'

Stress is the body's reaction to any demand made by it. It is psychological and physiological state that results when certain features of individual's environment, including noise, pressure, job promotions, monotony or the general climate. Experts quote stress as a factor in a wide variety of disease–hypertension, heart disease, diabetes, asthma, allergies, headache, fatigue, backache, skin disorder and so on. Frequent episodes of stress or distress keep the body in a state of chemical imbalance. The result of stress can be immediate like sleeplessness or heart disease (Dwivedi, R.S. 1997).

Work Place Injuries

One of the major health problems managers have complained about is backaches. Back injuries are the most prevalent of all work place injuries. They also are the most enigmatic. Since their exact causes and effects often remain a medical mystery. Chronic back disorders can develop gradually as a result of repetitive activity over time. Because of the slow onset and insidious character of these internal injuries, the condition often may be ignored until the symptoms become chronic. Acute back injuries usually are the immediate result of improper lifting of too heavy loading. Injuries can arise in muscle, tendon, and ligaments either singly or in combination.

Back injuries are expensive for all concerned. Back injury prevention measures and injury management programs for injured workers can reduce the human and financial impact of back pain. These include injury prevention, post-incidence, cost control, and back injury remedies (Saxena Pradeep, 2002).

HR Gains Prominence in Business Decisions

That's the finding of the annual human resource survey from Deloitte and Touché, Human Capital Advisory Service practice. The survey reveals that people-centred strategies relating to customer satisfaction, employee recruiting and talent retention are considered as integral part of achieving overall corporate success.

Launched in 1997, Deloitte and Touché periodic national survey of HR professionals identifies trends in human resources at fortune 1000 companies.

Moving beyond their role as transactional administrators, HR departments are evolving and gaining prominence as strategic business units. HR's role in contributing to employee satisfaction and retention remains paramount but the survey also reveals that HR has a new role in enhancing organizational profitability.

'Over the past 3 survey's, we've seen that HR professionals face an ever-growing range of responsibilities from attracting truly talented workers to ensuring their companies' success through major corporate initiatives and transformations,' said Richard Kleinert, global practice leader for HR strategic group of Deloitte and Touché. While HR functions have always been critical to ensuring overall success, this year the relationships between successful people strategies and business success is even more evident.

Key findings of the study:

- Customer Relationships demand strategy from HR. HR professionals are contributing to company wide relations, initially by linking assessment and selection, reward and learning company's overall customer relationship management strategy.
- HR professionals' still fighting the talent wars for best employees. The majority of HR professionals (92 per cent) find recruiting qualified employees a major issue even with a growing pool of available talent. HR professionals also noted that the needs to support employee motivation are increasing.
- Mergers and acquisitions often fail for lack of HR perspective of the HR professionals surveyed, the majority were involved in a merger in the last 2 years, but report that reviewing organizational performance measures, assessing communication methods and integrating compensation plans did not occur until the late stages of a merger. Instead HR professionals spent the early pre-merger days examining company demographics, collecting employee data and gathering information on policies and procedures (www.aviationcareer.net/hr).

Women Entrepreneurs

Cosmetic Executive Women is the prominent non-profit organization in Beauty Industry. As an organization for women, by women, their mission is three folds: further the professional development of their members, recognize achievement in the industry and to give charities that benefit women. As they began developing this resource for employees, managers, and HR departments that they too were at a loss for how to deal with an employee with cancer. The knowledge, skills, and attitudes of managers make a major difference in the work experience of employees undergoing treatment. Yet for these managers it was their first encounter with cancer. So after establishing a base set of resources for employees, including web site and printed materials, we created a plan to help managers manage through cancer. 'The managing through cancer program' this program was developed to focus on groups and interviews with employees, managers and HR executives.

The results obtained were such that in 2 years CEW foundation raised $ 1.5 million, to support this new initiative. While each company has faced these situations from time to time the HR managers believe that in all, it results in a better performance and bringing out the best from the present lot and with such a spirit intact most of the HR managers are busy devising strategies and systems to fight back fears and continue with their original goal (Carlotta Jacobson, 2002).

Recognizing HR as a Competitive Advantage

In knowledge based economy a company's competitive advantage is increasingly derived from human capital. Consequently, HR management will play a correspondingly critical role in attractive and retaining such valued employees and motivating them to achieve corporate objectives. In a 1999 qualitative study, which gathered view of 35 CEO's, line managers, and were found to be the key factors in determining the state of HR in organizations. 'Management Enlightenment' refers to the extent to which top management recognizes HR role in formulating and implementing company strategies. The failure of HR in playing a more strategic role can be attributed to lack of management enlightenment (www.gov.sg/mom/gen/mpn/000/index).

Human Resources Management and Human Relations

HR manager has a pivotal role to play in the HR manager process. Human resources manager is supposed to be a senior who has the capability not only to manage the human resources of the company, but to guide all the executives including the top boss. As he is directly reporting to the top boss, he must be able to keep the same wavelength with the boss, influencing and convincing him of the human resources policies, and ensuring his support for all the human resources development programmes.

He must be able to provide direction to all the functional resources philosophy that guide the process; and it is he who provides leadership to his subordinates in the HR function and other functional executives to adopt a human resources approach to management. The human resources manager may be actively involved in the HRM function in many respects.

- HR manager is supposed to formulate human resources policies and strategies and to plan HRM intervention in the whole organization.
- He is responsible too primarily to promote a HR philosophy all over the organization.
- He has to coordinate himself with the top management and obtain their approval and commitment for HRM strategies and development programs.
- He must be good educator, a good counselor who can conduct and supervise counseling sessions regularly.
- He must be a good communicator, who communicates with appropriate people, with appropriate information at the appropriate time in the most effective manner.
- He must be good leader who is able to establish teamwork and provide effective leadership.

- HRM manager must be a good human relationist and industrial relations man who maintains good and cordial industrial relations in his organization.
- HR manager must be able to for mullet and innersole effective human resources planning and integrate it and career planning.
- A good HR manager is the force behind establishing and maintaining teamwork team spent cohesion and a sense of belonging in the minds of people in the organization.
- He must maintain a well-planned supply line for appropriate manpower to various departments and functions.

In a nutshell it is the human resource manager's vision and commitment that guides the entire organization and it's functions and operation (Michael, V. P. 1999).

Characteristic of a Personnel Manager

Personnel manager has certain characteristics, which help him in his field of work. A personnel manager should be diplomatic and hold the employee's interest in new. It is important that he should have the active support of the top management. On the other hand, if he does not win the confidence of the employees and their union, the management will not respect him. Moreover, he has to earn the esteem of his colleagues especially those in the line who can be more interested in immediate rather than term results. He walks on a tight rope. Hence tact and imagination are his only guides.

To be successful in his job, a personnel manager should be a specialist in organization theory. Thinking he can advise top management in organizational matters while organizing his own department so as to minimize frictions, promote goodwill, and relieve the talent energies of his own people and associates.

He should be an expert in personnel administration, knowledge of relevant laws, procedure, technique, knowledge of economics, industrial psychology. He should have an adequate knowledge of behavioural science, which study the reactions of individuals and the group's top particular sets of condition and environments in an organization or a factory.

He should have a sense of social justice and fully appreciate the rights and interest of men and women at work and economic resection of management.

Other qualities include loyalty to the organization, honesty in his dealings with people; objectivity in judging the performance of people; sense of responsibility towards colleagues and subordinate and respect for the opinions of others.

He should be decisive and willing to make a decision and take a risk in doing so. He should have a capacity for persuasion, coupled with patience and tolerance.

The personnel manager therefore should have the capability to look to the following activities very efficiently keeping in view the requirement of efficient cooperation in the organization.

- Technical skill to accomplish the mechanics of a particular job.
- Human skills to build a team spirit on a leader.
- Conceptual skill to recognize the inter-relations involved in a situation to achieve the maximum good for the total organization.

Thus, the crucial task of a manager is that of leading, mobilizing and directing the efforts of those he manages (Subramani P.N. and G. Rajindra, 2001).

HR Management Tomorrow

The role of the HRD is expanding. Hence it is essential that HR managers be integrally involved, in the organizations strategic and policy-making activities. For example, in almost every one of the fortune 500 companies, the heard of the HRD is an officer (usually a vice-president) answering to the chief executive officer. In a significant number of companies the head of the HRD sits on either the board of directions or planning committee or both.

A survey conducted in 1980 by Opinion Research Corporation found that 69 per cent of the top managers and 73 per cent of HR managers surveyed expected the HR function to increase in importance over the next years.

If tomorrow's HR managers are to earn the respect of their colleagues and of top management they must work to overcome certain negative impressions biases sometimes associated with HRM. This can be accomplished in several ways.

- The HR specialist should become a more well redid businessperson. This will help overcome the common feeling that HR people don't understand the real problems and issues facing the organization.
- The HR managers should be fully knowledgeable about present and future trends and issues.
- The HR managers should promote effective HR utilization within the organization. They should stress the importance of positively impacting profit by effectively utilizing the organization's HR.
- The HR managers should help solve important organizational problems and should make suggestions that are practical and useful in meeting current organizational objectives.

In addition to performing the traditional HR functions, HR managers need to look for fresh and effective approaches to improving organizational performance. It has been suggested that HR manager should develop or refine their expertise in the following areas: attitude surveys and other upward communication problems, issues related to changing working conditions, job humanization, career planning and development, pay and benefits supplemental uses of the workplace and flexible work schedules.

The primary goal of HR management in any organization is to facilitate organizational performance one of the most effective ways of doing this is by increasing productivity. HR managers have limited impact on capital materials and energy aspects of productivity. However they have great impact on labour capital. Thus they can affect employee commitment and management philosophy of individual managers (Hord L.Byars and Hestile W. Rue. 1987).

Qualities of HRM Manager

The HRM/Personnel manager is caught between the conflicting interests of management and labour, weighted down by his/her loyalty to the management and duties to the workers; subjected to political and bureaucratic hassles, ruthlessly cross-examined in courts, scorched by the glare of occasional publicity the HRM/ personnel manager does not have one permanent image. It changes from one set to another set of people and from one situation to another. To the aggrieved and oppressed labour he is the management's henchman, self-serving and unscrupulous. To the enraged trade union he is the villain of the piece, holding back an acceptable settlement, and a representative of the exploiting class; to the unsuccessful job seekers, he is the corrupt officer.

The functions of HRM give us some idea of the qualities, which a successful HR manager must possess. The most important quality is his ability is deal successfully with people who have favour home and are prejudicial against others. He has to deal with workers who refuse to see reason and who believe that violence pays, and nothing else does. The other qualities are stated below.

A HR manager should be fair in matter of promotions, demotions, transfers, day- off and be form in enforcing discipline. He should be tactful in dealing with difficult situations. He should have resourceful adjustability to tackle a difficult matter from different angles.

The HR manager must be guided by sympathetic attitude toward employee demands. Some demands are unreasonable but patient listening, open mind and concern for employee's welfare make reluctant worker relent.

The HR manager must possess a sound knowledge of constitution and other acts which influence labour interest. He should have a broad social outlook and contribute towards the betterment of the quality of life of the employees and those who live around and beyond the company.

The HR manager must have competence to perform activities relating to personnel better than his subordinate must. He must have a long-term perspective as to map out a future for the organization 15-20 years ahead and even beyond.

Communication skill is quality, which the HR manager must be endowed with. He should be quick at decision making selfless and have character. Character refers to the quality of completing what has commenced, living upped promises and expects aprons and acting as a role model for others (Aswapthappa K. 1997).

Personnel Managers' Attitude Towards Their Profession

The objective of the study (Jayaraman K. 1996) was to find out how organizational hierarchy affects the personnel managers in their attitude towards their profession. 760 personnel managers were given the questionnaire out of which 115 responded.

115 personnel managers working in different industries in Tamil Nadu were studied for their attitude towards their profession. The results indicated that the managerial level or educational level or the kind of management in the industries does not influence the attitude of personnel managers. However personnel managers are differing in their attitudes towards their profession when they were grouped into different clusters using cluster analysis.

HRM Practices in Equal Employment Opportunity

This research (Konrad, et al. 1995) examined whether the employment status of women and minorities in an organization is associated with the presence of formalized human resources management (HRM) in that company. The antecedents and outcomes of formalized HRM structures were studied in 138 organizations by assessing the presence of identity blind and identity conscious (those taking demographic identities into account) HRM structure. HRM vice-presidents completed questionnaires. Findings indicated that identity conscious structures were associated with some positive indicators of the employment, status of women and people of colour. Top managers – attitudes were significant predictors of effective equal opportunity efforts. It is concluded that such practices, although perhaps adopted for symbolic purposes, improved the employment status of protected groups.

Human Resource Managers and Firm's Performance

This study (Snell, Scott A, and Voundt, Mark A, 1995) brought out as to how the approach human resource managers take towards HRM is related to changes in the financial performance of their firms, as assessed by return on assets on sales growth. The results from 102 single product firms indicated that the firm performance was higher when the approach to HRM was based on behaviour control, and when managers had complete knowledge of cause-effect relations. HRM based output control had neither a direct nor a moderating effect on firm performance. When the approach to HRM was based on input control, performance was higher when standards of desirability were ambiguous. Thus, behavioural and input approaches offer the most potential as a basis for improving performance through HRM.

HRM and Turnover

The research (Huselid, Mark A, 1995) evaluated the links between systems of high performance work practices (HPWP) and firm performance. HPWP includes comprehensive employee recruitment and selection procedures, incentive, compensation and performance management systems, extensive employee involvement, and training. Human resource professionals at 968 firms completed questionnaires on HPWP; internal and external fit, turnover, productivity, and financial performance, control variables included size, growth in sales and levels of profitability.

Results indicated that HPWP practices had an economically and statistically significant impact on both intermediate employee outcomes (turnover and productivity) and short and long term measures of corporate financial performance.

HRM and the Appropriation

This research discussed the concept of 'appropriation' in explaining the underlying ethos and rationale in human resource management practice, which the authors contend is largely underpinned by the objective of appropriating the human resource 'value'. The traditional approach to appropriation is characterized by such concerns as skill formation, commitment to the organization, shared corporate values and a reliance on formally constituted governance structures with a putative integrating ethos. This paper advocates a reconstitution of the appropriation regime to incorporate the concepts of knowledge and learning. The authors draw from the innovation management literature to highlight the problematic nature of appropriation and to clarify the implications of appropriation to the management of the knowledge that resides in people. They also suggest how future research might proceed within an appropriation – learning perspective (Kamoche Ken and Mueller Frank, 1998).

HRM and Diversity Initiatives

As more and more organizations implement diversity initiatives, personnel and human resource managers play increasingly significant roles. This article explores some of the challenge personnel and human resource manager face, implementing 'diversity'. It discusses strategy personnel and human resource managers are employing to address the need for diversity as a principle of human resource management (HRM). These strategies include processes such as diversity audits to identify organizational problems, aligning workplace, and workforce planning, benchmarking personnel, and positioning diversity as a top-level management function. The article also examines the benefits of flex management and educating and training managers / line supervisors to effectively manage diversity (Mathews Audrey, 1998).

New Industrial Relations and HR Policies

As a result of the new economic policies, IR and HRM have acquired strategic importance. The success of the new policies would depend to a large extent on the introduction of new industrial relations and human resource policies at the national and enterprise levels some measure for change has already been witnessed in the IR and Human Resource Manager's areas. The actors of the system now realize that neither the economy nor the industrial enterprises can survive by clinging to the rigid posture. Therefore the discussion of the actors are now centred around how to change and in what direction.

This article*(Indian Journal of Industrial Relations, 1994)* examines and highlights some specific challenges, pressures for bringing about change in industrial relations and human resource managers, and suggests future policy directions in their areas.

Competition also necessitates improving the quality of products, reduction in costs to be able to sell competitive prices. All this requires a workforce who is trained, motivated, and committed, these are not ordinary tasks. Nonetheless while training can be imparted, it is not true of seeking motivation and commitment of the employees. This may be achieved through the philosophy and practices of the management, which are oriented for HRD and the welfare of the employee.

Human Resource Management for Tomorrow

The economy and the policy of India is first changing in the wake of the liberalization policies mooted by Rajiv Gandhi goverment. and formalized by Narasimha Rao government. Consequently the form of production has undergone a change. What has emerged is a new era in human resource management. This article imagines this field in the years to come.

Focus of this article is on a model of human resource management as what will be relevant in the Indian economy and policy during the first part of this century. By then the liberalized policy would have bad effect global pressure for an increased competitiveness would have mounted and human resource management would be more clearly seen as conjunction of business policy towards capital and labour. Today's industrial relations manager has emerged as executive who is as important if not more then the financial controller, the production manager, material manager, or the maintenance manager. His position in the years going to be more important and so are his needs to be efficient, effective and get competitive edge from his human resource which will make the difference between success and failure. For this human resource expert has to have global vision, a keen foresight, and an aptitude to influence and direct change. He than becomes the reason, and a catalyst of organizational changes (*Indian Journal of Industrial Relations,* 1994).

Human Resource Management Practices

The direct investment of multinational corporations (MNCs) in the South Asia and its influence in the economic development of this region in the last decade have been focused in national and international conferences and in business school seminars. The importance of human resource management practices on firm effectiveness and economic growth in this region is evident. Yet research and international HRM particularly in this region has emerged only recently although studies in general management practices in various countries. Despite a long history of international foreign operations in this studies focused on human resource management clearly depicts all these factors (*Indian Journal of Industrial Relations,* 1994a).

Human Resources and Public Sector Reform

Since the term first coined in 1950s development administration has been seen as focusing on the change involved in implementing policies of economic and social development. Parallel with this has been less widely acknowledged interest in the change needed within the organization if they are to maximize their effectiveness in bringing about change. Some of the human resource implications of this have been picked up in the human resource development literature, which stress that highlights of education and health are both means to and a measure of the success of development policies.

This article takes a step further arguing for the centrality of a strategic human resource approach to the management of a public sector organizations as an essential reform if the contribution of such administrative agencies to the achievement of the objective of social and economic (Michael Hess, 1995).

The Necessity of Change Process

In his book *Getting the Right People* Kesho Prasad discusses the necessity and the mechanism of change process. Business people, all the companies from all the sectors face the reorganization plans, and are responding quickly to competition, establishing new products and markets and adapting themselves to fluctuations in the economy. The management of Human Resources has attained prime importance in view of changed scenario where a developing country like India is facing stiff competition while going global in the areas of quality, productivity, and efficiency. The book serves as good guideline for both theoretical and practical approaches adopted by contemporary industrial organizations. The book emphasizes the fact that emerging trends in HRD have to be integrated with the business plans of the organization.

The author maintains that there are a number of books on human resource management dealing not with Indian situation. The book serves as good guideline for both theoretical and practical approaches adopted by contemporary industrial organizations. The book emphasizes the fact that emerging trends in HRD have to be integrated with the business plans of the organization.

The book (Prasad Kesho, 2000) is divided into eleven chapters. In the first chapter of the book author has presented the historical perspectives. Starting point of the concept in the second chapter " Growth of personnel management in India." Focusing on conditions in which it has emerged. In the 3rd and 4th chapter what is the current or present pictures. The importance of human resource is discussed. In the following chapter the author suggests guidelines on giving and receiving motivation in dealing with people of different attitudes, one of the hallmarks of a good human resource manager. Chapters 7, 8, 9 deal with clarifying goals getting and using information and facts weighing pros and cons being rational and arriving at a decision quickly. Other chapters point on motivating the people, gathering creativity using experiences recognizing a good idea and a good person building a network for career enhancement.

This book provides managers with a comprehensive and insightful overview written in an immensely readable style and replete with examples. The language of the book is very lucid and explicit. This book will be of interest to practicing managers trainer, consultants and to those who want to realize their real self.

HR Managers–Manage Your Stress

Everyone has to cope with stress at some time but HR managers have to be specially careful to seek ways of reducing it by working within reasonably well defined areas as agreed with the management team and deciding on their priorities, roles and tasks. This will help to reduce role strain and role overload. Some ways to do this are:

- Get plenty of exercise and sleep
- Eat healthy food
- Take breaks and relax
- Use humor to reduce a tense situation
- Acquire a wide range of skills
- Set realistic deadlines
- Develop hobby and value friendship

If a situation becomes too stressful, it is best to discuss the situation with a member of the management team (Hargreaves P and Jarvis P. 1997).

Manager's Guide to Health and Safety at Work

Most managers in organization are now aware of their legal obligations as far as health and safety is concerned. According to the European Union Legislation, employers must ensure that working practices do not result in injury to staff- Assure visual display units (VDUs) do not cause eyestrain.

- Ensure that noise levels are acceptable.
- Ensure safety of all electrical and mechanical equipment.
- Transport materials, gases, and liquids, safely.
- Provide protecting equipment and clothing.
- Undertake risk assessment on wide range.

Everyone should have a health and safety responsibility towards his or her colleagues. Staff developers should obtain up-to-date regulations so they can organize training events. Well-qualified advisors should provide courses (Stranks J. 1997).

Liberalization and Human Resource Management

In this book, chaptèr one deals with the programmes of economic liberalization adopted in India, reform package, and its implications for Human Resource Management. The authors feel that the order of the day has now become "survival of the fittest" resulting in the closure, takeover, or sale of inefficient units. It necessitates a cultural shift in work practices at the enterprise level, which has to focus on employee efficiency, skill upgradation including multi-skill, induction of new technology, benchmarking HR practices, and adoption of learner and flatter organizational structure.

Organizational restructuring which has become a prerequisite for contemplating various human resource mechanisms and strategies in Indian companies is discussed in chapter 2. Delaying, downsizing, mergers, and alliances are some of the issues dealt in this section. Changing role of the HR department has also been prescribed here in short, and it has been suggested that it should be distinct from the administrative function, and goals and responsibilities of the HR department. It should be defined in a tangible and measurable way. This, however, appears to be most difficult for most Indian organizations to date.

Parts 3 and 5 of the book provide insights on managing change through continuous improvement and corporate strategy and human resource management. One fails to understand which corporate strategy and HRM are presented later while these are of paramount importance today. The term HRM itself signifies Strategic Human Resource Management (SHRM). But most Indian literature on this subject fails to impart this meaning; rather they give an expanded meaning to the Traditional Personnel Management (TPM) which is akin to 'old wine in a new bottle.'

Labour policy issues are discussed in chapter 4 of the book. Voluntary retirement scheme and worker-management relationships are the major issues. Chapter 6 is the last and presents the recipe for the human resource management in 2020. How to deal with the information technology imperative in coming times and the emergence of the concept of virtual organization are also presented in this book. Diversity management is also discussed in short.

The book ends up highlighting issues pertaining to the social responsibility of the business thus reinforcing the view that human resource management is nothing but an endeavour towards providing quality of work life (QWL) to the people and at large the quality of life (Engineer Arun M. 1999).

HR Professionals in a Changing Business Environment

The importance of human resource function and HR professionals has grown after the realization that 'people' aspect really matters, and it can make a difference, and it will focus more on organizational performance, and it will move into a leadership position, as organizations come to know how much they depend on it. HR professionals have to look for opportunities to acquire influence within the world of organization and to make top management understand the importance of 'human resources.' HR professionals' competencies would also change with their role. They have to develop a mixture of competencies such as functional knowledge and diagnostic skills, strong self-concept, personal influence, tactical planning, and results orientation. The goal of HR would be to integrate the company's business processes with its people processes. HR professionals' biggest job will be to think and act like business people. HR professionals will also be concerned with women workforce, their place in organization, pay disparity, and lack of corporate concern to family obligation.

The issues of how to integrate and promote women in the workplace, and how to make workplace more women-friendly are urgent. Health care will be another concern for HR managers with continued growth of medical cost, expansion of managed care, and difficulties associated with the aging of baby-boom generation. Demographic shift will force a change in the way HR thinks about staffing–how to retain, manage and deploy an aging workforce. HR managers have to think how to keep middle aged workers productive and satisfied, as advancement opportunities to reach top management level may not be available to them all.

The HR professionals have to adopt a three–tier strategy to be successful at the global, organizational and individual levels. At the global level, HR strategy should be adopted after exploring the larger social, cultural, economic and technical environments, which affect the workforce dynamics. At the organizational level HR professionals have to align HR strategy with organizational performance and growth, and they should develop innovative HR practices and policies accordingly. At the individual level, HR function may be related to identify and develop such competencies through training, education and development programs as required by individuals to increase their performance and change their behaviour in expected direction.

Also in general, there are four ways in which the work of human resources can be changed:

Restructuring HR bureaucracy, looking at HR ratio, that is number of HR professionals per the number of employees.

Automation and application of technology to dissolve the routine administrative work placed on the profession.

Outsourcing HR work to improve service delivery to employees in the organization.

Redesign HR work to be faster, better and cheaper.

In sum, HR professionals will need a range of competencies to succeed in future by playing the role of a strategic business partner, who leverage human capital and expert knowledge for competitive advantage?

The role of HR professionals in new paradigm of business is to be redefined as the next millennium has set a very challenging task for HR managers. HR profession has changed due to changes taking place in business caused by global competition, downsizing and technological advances. HR professionals are in a great flux due to workplace and socio-cultural changes taking place across the globe. The corporate world wants HR managers to play the role of catalyst, at the same time they also want them to cope up with the problems, and issues related to workforce. The millennium will witness the birth and evolution of HR profession from confrontational industrial relations to strategies human resource development. The importance of human resource function and HR professionals has grown after the realization that 'people' aspect really matters, and it can make a difference. HR will focus more on organizational performance and it will move into a leadership position as organizations come to know how much they depend on it.

HR professionals will also be concerned with women workforce, their place in organization, lack of promotion to senior management, pay disparity and lack of corporate concern to family obligation (Srivastava K. B.L. 2000).

Human Resources Management for the India of Tomorrow

According to the argument, HRM could be described as a line function, which facilitates the interaction between the owners of capital and the owners of labour power so that the objective function of the organization is optimized. This means that in future organization and status charts will depict the human resource manager to be par with the production manager and the finance manager. Thus HRM is an activity that should not and cannot be viewed in isolation. It is a part of the total environment, and is conditioned by it. Three sets of influences, which condition the form, and content of business policy towards capital and labour are given.

The first sets of influences, which impinge on the HRM function, are the exogenous variables. The three chief variables are:

- The product market (be it is the goods sector, the commodities sector or the service sector).
- The capitalist State (be it either a metropolis or a satellite). The states performs two kinds of roles: (a) the family, the religion and social mores. (b) The repressive role fulfilled by such bodies as the armed forces, the police, and the judiciary.
- The multinational corporation. It is an economy within an economy and a living example of a micro-macro synthesis.

The second set of variables could be described as endogenous variables. The three factors here are:

- The Company History: What kind of policies and practices has come down the years as accepted normal working practice.
- The Employee Collectivity. (Such as trade unions as well as an unorganized body of employees uniting over particular issues)
- The organization may be out-dated with changing functions and technology. With this human relationships will also change. This kind of change lies at the heart of such issues as trust faith, loyalty, and responsibility. Chain of common and anti of authority are aspects of this function.

The third set of variables is Ideological Influences. These include three main factors:

- Corporate culture, which is based on company history, vision of the helmsman and the ideology of the Board.
- Corporate ethics based on the belief systems as well as the manner in which management and union view objective social reality.

- The importance of state ideology cannot be under-played.

This sum is what HRM has come to imply in the 1990's and what it will be seen as in the years to come. Power, control, class relations, and alienation, all the facets find their place in the modern day conceptualization of HRM.

HRM has come to occupy the centre stage and it is going to remain there for a long time to come. But this will top echelons of management are convinced that a re-definition of the role of the Human Resource Manager is necessary. And all such change must of necessity come from the top downwards. Grass roots activity would remain only as a feedback mechanism and will not be able to bring about change on its own (Sorab Sadri and Pranabesh Ray, 1993).

Leadership Styles and Problem Solving Behaviour

The study attempted to explore into the leadership and problem solving styles of executives of a public organization. A stratified random sample of 150 middle level executives was administered a Creative Problem Solving Inventory and a Managerial Style Questionnaire.

It was hypothesized that in the Indian context middle level managers would dominantly use authoritative, democratic and coaching styles. It was also hypothesized that problem solving styles and leadership styles were independent of each other.

Understanding the nature and type of problem solving and leadership styles prevalent among its executives is very useful to an organization, because the management of an organization achieves its objectives by utilizing all the resources effectively and efficiently. Among all the resources, human resource plays a vital role.

It is found that the nurturing and task oriented leadership styles as well as characteristics of autonomy and interaction in the job, contributed positively to the overall effectiveness rate of leaders (Panchanatham N. and Karuppiah K. R. K. 1993).

Qualifications of HR Manager

The functions of HR manager vary from organization to the other both in nature and degree. So, the qualifications required of HR manager too differ from one organization to another. In general, qualifications and qualities can be summarized as:

Personal Attributes

HR must have initiative, resourcefulness, and depth of perception, maturity in judgement and analytical ability. He must have intellectual integrity, freedom from bias, should be through with labour laws, and must have an understanding of human behaviour. HR should also possess other personal attributes like:

(i) **Intelligence**–This includes skills to communicate, articulate, moderate, understand etc, command over language, mental ability and tact in dealing with people intelligently etc, ability to draft agreements, policies etc.

(ii) **Educational Skills**–HR manager should possess learning and teaching skills, as he has to learn and teaching employees about organizational growth etc.

(iii) **Discriminating Skills**–HR manager should have the ability to discriminate between right and wrong, just and unjust, merit and demerit.

(iv) **Executing Skills**–HR manager expected to execute the management decisions regarding personnel issue with speed, accuracy, and objective.

(v) **Leadership Qualities**–HR manager is expected to have deep faith in human values, empathy with human problems, foreseeing future needs of employees, organization, government, trade union etc.

Experience and Training

Previous experience in an appropriate environment and area is an advantage. Training in psychological aspects, labour, legislation, personnel management is an additional benefit– which helps towards an appreciation of the general management problems and a practical approach in meeting personal problems.

Professional Attitudes

Is it more necessary in Indian context? The HR manager's job is getting professionalized. He should have patience and understanding, ability to listen before offering advice. He must have patience and understanding, ability to listen before offering advice. He must have knowledge of various disciplines. He must be able to couple his social justice with a warm personal interest in people, which must be secured by an uncommon degree of common sense.

Qualifications

Qualifications prescribed for the post of HR manager may vary from industry to industry and from state to state and these have been undergoing several changes from time to time (P. Subba Rao, 2000).

The Art of HRD in Staff Development

The idea that managers and supervisors should be responsible for training and development of their people is still fairly new but rapidly gaining influences. Their involvement in development of human resources is important for various reasons.

First, leadership means influencing behaviour of other people positively. One of the best ways of supporting staff members is by helping them improve their knowledge and skills. To do this manager need to encourage continuous learning and improvement on the job.

Second, most problems boil down to 'people problems'. If the managers list the problems and analyze the same, most of them are often related to poor communication among the staff, lack of training or immature attitudes. By ensuring that their staffs are trained and helping them to develop their skills, managers can solve many of their 'people problems'.

Third, many organizations are encouraging their managers and supervisors to become more proactive and less bureaucratic. Decision-making is pushed down the line. Staff training and development is also one aspect of this proactive approach and a way of generating more initiative and flexibility in the people.

Training should be in areas of how to solve problems, and respond to situations themselves.

Fourth, in order to be effective staff training and development needs to be linked with the job and involve employees, managers and supervisors. Their involvement should reduce the possibilities of conflict and frustration. It should also help employees to transfer their newly acquired knowledge and skills to the actual jobs they do also the power of managers as 'boss' can also be harnessed.

Finally, staff development is not a new responsibility, HR managers are already spending a considerable amount of their time and energy on activities related to staff development:

- Discuss future work with their employees
- Introduce a new person to the department
- Get one person to show another how to do something
- Conduct a staff meeting or team discussion
- Delegate work and responsibilities
- Coach one of the employees and provide some guidance
- Conduct a performance review meeting

Indeed staff training and development is one of the key functions and responsibilities of managers. Unless the human resources are not made capable and responsible organizational goals cannot be achieved (Peter Sheal, 1999).

Human Resource Professionals in Managing Change

If indeed human resource professionals have to grow and develop into becoming business partners within the organization, they need to take the lead in managing change. The business environment today is ever changing in terms of technologies, market, and industry. This calls for proactive and business oriented human resource management, which perpetually keeps an organization on its toes and prevents complacency. An organization in which people are complacent resting on past laurels and taking customers is dangerous but familiar situation.

Instead of feeling secure about the present, individuals should constantly be on guard and be looking ahead, only then can change be possible.

To achieve this, Kotter in his book *Leading Change* suggests that 'creating' a crisis when time is good can effectively trigger people off on the right track by creating a financial loss, by setting very high targets for sales revenue and productivity. Though this appears to be a harsh measure, it can shake people out of their complacency get them charged up, thus bringing about change in the outlook and work attitude.

Any change from a set pattern evokes fear about the uncertainty that lies ahead. Thus transformation has to be dealt with carefully and converted into an opportunity. Corporate leaders and human resource strategist have to take up this challenge changing work attitudes across the organization. This involves guiding leading, enabling and motivating people.

The colour and complexion of industry has changed due to changes in technology and expansion of world markets. While organizations in the past had relatively stable and predictable environments, today's organizations have to cope with the unexpected. The development of a positive works culture, where employees work as teams, is perhaps one of the best ways to manage change and role of HR manager plays a key role in this.

A study by Roberts for measuring business performance has pinpointed how strategic HRM can improve performance and increase profits. The study gives an insight into how a well-defined human resource strategy can transform a business into a profitable venture.

Participation of management: an increase up to 15 per cent in profitability is possible if managerial participation in decision making and business strategy is increased.

Open style of management: an increase in profitability of 28 per cent is possible if all levels of management are unanimous about the need to change. Further, if people are 'open', it clearly makes a lot of difference.

Delegating risk-taking powers to managers: managers should be empowered to take rises to get results. Managers, in turn, should follow a middle of the road approach to balance the benefits approach to balance the benefits and dangers of risk taking.

Composition of top management team: small businesses have been found to achieve higher profitable with the recruitment of high percentage of new blood or employees; where home - as larger organizations require more experienced, home – grown managers.

Training of managers: there is a direct correlation between training and profitability, especially in companies committing sufficient days a year towards training.

Incentives for top management: this helps to generate greater performance however; the impact of inventive can vary with the level of manager.

Succession planning: a formal succession planning system is a ritual element for building an organization, which has the inherent, and reinvents itself. This can be achieved by identifying, grooming and empowering successors as part of the job description.

Performance appraisal: a professional well oriented, appraisal system considerably enhances both individual and company performance (Monappa Arun and Mahrukh Engineer, 2000).

HR Profession in India

As a developing country, the need for effective utilization of resources, and increased professionalism is being called for in management of human resources.

Guided by the need to have factual data on the current trends and changes influencing the personnel function, a national survey was undertaken. Major areas covered by the survey were perspectives and challenges, education and training, structure, contents and process, the role of NIPM (National Institute of Personnel Management).

This survey was conducted to identify and evaluate the relative importance of issues converting HR profession. The questionnaire was administered to every third corporate member of NIPM. Over 2,800 questionnaires were mailed across the country in different organizations at different states to HR professionals at various levels out of which 402 responses were complete in all aspects were accepted for final analysis.

Most respondents belong to the age group of 36-40 years (21 per cent) and only 9.87 per cent were more than 56 years of age. 98 per cent were males and less than 20 per cent were females. Most of the respondents belonged to middle level in their organizations (58.38 per cent, 33.0 per cent) working at top levels and 8.38 per cent working at junior levels. 73.70 per cent of respondents were employed by multi-unit organization as compared to 26.30 per cent employed single unit organizations.

- The prioritized factors affecting HR professionals are technological change, concern for quality, productivity, and the increasing profile of educated workforce.
- The major hurdle for the HR professionals in their effective performance is the lack of top management support and lack adequate and meaningful research inputs to the profession.
- Respondents were least satisfied with regard to the interaction between academics and organizations. The course curricula and subjects were generally satisfactory.
- High level of dissatisfaction prevails with regard to quality of students' fieldwork placement and projects, due to lack of seriousness and ineffective monitoring of such projects by organizations.
- The reading habits of HRM professionals are generally very good.
- The HR professionals are by and large satisfied with the nature of work and least satisfied with the career growth opportunities.
- They are called upon to do work that does not fall under the purview of the HR function significantly, some do all the work not related to HR function at all.

- Most of their work time is spent in meeting individuals in discussion, negotiations, counseling, liaison etc
- The major work area has been the Industrial Relations, managing the work discipline and handling grievances.
- Completely computerized Personnel information system (PIS) has been adopted by very few organizations and in most of them only a partial attempt has been made.
- On the role of NIPM (National Institute of Personnel Management), a strong filling exists that the interaction among the NIPM HQ, Office Bearers and the members need to be improved and that certain professional values and ethics need to be brought into the profession. The assessment of the institute in terms of its organization has been only average (Akhilesh K.B. and R. Sekar, 2000).

HR Manager as a Specialist

The personnel department has staff relationship with other departments. It is responsible for advising management from managing director to the lowest line supervisor on all areas relating to personnel management and industrial relations. It also performs various functions of employment, training, and development.

The HR manager must exercise control very tactfully in order to win the confidence and co-operation of all line managers. The authority of HR manager should derive from concrete personnel policies and programmes and from the advantage and result of accepted specialized knowledge.

As a source of help: in certain situations, experienced HR managers assume line responsibility for personnel matters. But they should earn the reputation and confidence of line managers of being a source of help rather than a source of threat to them.

As a change agent: HR manager should work as an enabler and change agent regarding personnel areas and should be familiar with different disciplines like management, technology, sociology, psychology and organizational adaptability, viable and development are dependent on HRD. So the HR manager should work as a consultant of an organizational development by providing necessary inform and infrastructure to line manager.

As a controller: nevertheless, it is still true that effective personnel executives advise on policies, HMP managers in implementing their programmes, provide service, and exercise function sparingly.

From this, one can conclude that role of HR manager, as a specialist is indeed versatile! (Rao P. Subba 2000).

The HRD Missionary

The following are the essential qualities for an HRD missionary to be successful:

- *Person of positive thinking with positive attitudes to people:* An HRD manager needs to be positive person or a person with positive thinking. A positive person is one who is an optimistic, respects other people to make things happen, has an attitude to approach problems and issues with an open mind and hope of success, and believes that people can develop at any stage of their life. He/she has to the problems and frustrations of others. He/she should therefore have abundant positive energy to absorb these without losing his own faith and positivism and at the same time inspire others.
- *A high desire to learn:* He should be a person who is constantly looking for learning opportunities and using them. He should not be a person who thinks that he knows everything about HRD but a person who is interested in discovering more and more about it.
- *Interest in people:* He should be interested in meeting people within his own organization and outside and should have an attitude to treat every transaction as a learning opportunity. Associated with this quality is a listening capability. The HRD manager should be a good listener.
- *Helpful attitude:* He should have the great desire to help others and to be of service to others. He should have high

"Extension Motivation" a desire to serve others and work for larger goals.

- *Initiative taking or proactivity:* He should be a proactive person always willing to take the initiative, with a certain amount of risk taking and creativity.
- *Practice and perseverance:* As HRD managers are required to design, introduce, and monitor systems, they need to have a high degree of patience and perseverance to implement systems.
- *Communication skills:* HRD managers are required to be in constant touch with the line managers and other staff. They have to inspire them by actions and influence them through constant communication.
- *Objectivity approach:* HRD staffs need to be people with high degree of objectivity and fewer biases about others. They should not be the "judging" types of people. They should be able to treat every employee with respect. They should have high degree of faith in the capacity of human beings to change and develop.
- *Personal example and sense of discipline:* HRD managers should be willing to set personal examples for others, discipline in approach and be willing to sacrifice personal goals for organizational or larger group goals. The mission of the HRD manager is to build such a climate in the organization and simultaneously bring about a change in the thinking of individuals.

The HRD manager's job has many traps and temptations. Some of these are by virtue of the nature of the HRD function, some others are due to the structuring of the job, and a few others are due to the human nature. An awareness of the traps and temptations, a periodic introspection and renewal may go a long way in helping HRD managers to avoid these traps and temptations.

A frequent temptation HRD staff face, may be their need to support the top management and their decisions in order to maintain good relations with top management. Sometimes the

HRD staff tends to do it at the cost of their relationships and credibility with line managers. The HRD staff should have the courage to stand up and point out the problems and issues rather than blindly supporting the top management. He should not sacrifice HRD values and be prepared to face temporary inconveniences. Some other traps are means—end traps, power traps, empire building trap, administration trap, and insulation trap and development stagnation trap (Rao, T.V. 1990).

Integrated HRD Approach

HR professional's role, is taking a different shape, and is continuously expanding. Value addition to human resources is becoming the key for an organization's survival and growth. It must be clear that "human resources", we mean the day-to-day transaction among human beings within and outside an organization that prepares an individual towards realizing and achieving the goals of an industry as a part of a team. It is therefore, the practice and not the theory that is important. The need of the day is a radical transformation in the practice of human resource management.

Human resource managers today should have a complete understanding of the business functions and be familiar with its process beginning from raw material procurement and resource deployment to sales of products and collection. It is understood that while doing this. HR manager themselves will become familiar to the workmen and will be perceived as value creator and problem solver rather than overhead statistics. It is also necessary for them to transform "production workers" to "knowledge workers," who are capable of perceiving needs of the customers and catering to them at their level. Thus knowledge becomes a tool in the hands of the HR manager which has to be retained, upgraded, disseminated and applied. This is a complex process since they must deal with diverse groups having different approaches, ideas, and perceptions. HR managers must be able to arrive at a synthesis after considering the existing differences on various people related issues for achieving synergy for growth and development.

We must say that HR management, as it is practiced in India, suffers from a major drawback. It is biased in favour of the management. By 'biased' we do not mean that it tries to benefit the management alone, but that its focus has been managerial. Development of this field requires that both – management and employee – perspectives receive equal attention on HR professionals.

This basic principle has to be understood by HR managers and through them, by all the employees, and only then the desired change can be brought about. However a word of caution is that: change may not always benefit all employees, but as long as it benefits a majority and a deserving majority, HR management is on the right track. We therefore could conclude by reiterating that HR has to play a major role in formulating and implementing business strategy, as it adds value to the most important resource, i.e., the human resource (Sastry M.B.S., 1999).

Management Technology and the Role of HRD

Transfer of management technology is viewed as changes in the ability to improve the functioning of enterprises. Effective transfer, however, depends on an understanding of current managerial practices of local enterprises as well as on how user organizations can change to manage productivity functioning. The concept of transfer of management technology is, thus, intimately linked to the ability to manage technology and organizational behaviour. It has been established through research that all technology transfer constitutes organizational change. As such, it has been questioned whether technology transfer can occur without the active involvement of people within the change setting. This has resulted in the need to consider human resource development (HRD) as a significant part of the technology transfer process. Of all the individual activities related to HRD, nations differ in how they view their work environments, and these differences can be grouped into clusters of countries.

A substantial amount of this research, conducted from international comparative management and cross-cultural perspectives, supports the assertion that national boundaries and cultural identities also account for certain responses, independent of job level and work group. This paper attempts to explain the influence and effect of certain factors and patterns that are responsible for the effective and efficient transfer of management technology across national borders. A conceptual model is proposed based on the analysis of relevant literature and findings of an empirical investigation, to explain the effects and implications of the factors on the transfer process.

'People' is the most important and valuable resources every organization has in the form of its employees. Dynamic people can build dynamic organizations. Effective employees can contribute to the effectiveness of the organization. Therefore, organizations should continuously ensure that the dynamism, competency, motivation, and effectiveness of the employees remain at high levels. Human Resource Development is thus a continuous process to ensure the development of employee competencies, dynamism, motivation, and effectiveness in a systematic and planned way.

In some organizations there is no separate HRD department but there is only HRD manager. The HRD manager's role is integrated into personnel manager's job and the HRD function is integrated into the personnel function. HRD manager refers to any employee of an organization or institution that has some formally designated responsibilities to facilitate the development of others. Therefore, all HRD staff is included in this definition (Gani A. Ahad M. Osman, 1996).

HRD Managers or Departments

Play a crucial role in the organization. They perform a variety of functions such as:

- Role analysis
- HR planning
- Recruitment
- Selection

- Placement
- Induction
- Performance appraisal
- Training
- Management development
- Career planning and development
- Organizational development
- Compensation
- Social and cultural
- Workers' participation in management
- Quality circles
- Employee counseling
- Teamwork
- Communication policies
- Monetary and non-monetary rewards
- Employee benefits
- Grievance mechanism

Others functions of HRD managers include:

- Developing a human resource philosophy for the entire organization
- Influence personnel policies
- To plan and design new HRD methods
- Inspiring the line managers
- Monitor effectively the implementation of various HRD methods
- To conduct human process research organizational health surveys and renewal of exercises periodically
- To work with unions and associations and inspire them.

Attributes of HRD manager: According to Pareek and Rao, HRD manager must possess the following attributes:

Technical

- Knowledge of various types of performance appraisal system and ability to develop them.
- Knowledge of various types of tests and measurements of behaviour.
- Ability to design and execute training programmes at various levels.
- Knowledge of career planning and other personnel practices.
- Knowledge of behavioural sciences.
- Knowledge and skills in counseling.
- Understanding of overall organizational culture.
- Knowledge of techniques in behavioural research.

Managerial

- Organizing ability
- System development skills

Personality

- Initiative
- Faith in human beings and their capabilities
- Positive attitude towards others
- Imagination and creativity
- Concern for excellence
- Concern for people and their development
- Friendly, sociable and affable
- Attitude for research and developing work
- Interest in learning new things
- Ability to work as a team member (Rao P. Subba 2000).

Challenges Faced by HRD Managers

HRD managers are facing many challenges. Some of them are:

- *Enlarging the scope of personnel management*–Today, the scope has enlarged to include every activity in the organization, which has a human dimension.

- ***Focus on Knowledge and Skill***–The success of an organization depends on the knowledge and skills of its people. Hence, their knowledge and skills should be developed.
- ***Structure and Size of Enterprise***–Employees of MNC's come from different countries and nations having dissimilar culture, philosophy, and value systems. Managing a group of heterogeneous people throw greater challenges to modern managers.
- ***Managerial Skills in HRD***–Management of human resource requires special skills because it is a complex job. HR manager must be able to predict employee's behaviour. While meeting the expectations of employees to motivate them manager must also ensure organizational objectives are not sacrificed. Success of manager depends on the unique way in which he is able to motivate each employee. In managing people, the best technique is to love them. Trust and love increase morale, motivation, and efficiency. It also improves sense of belongings and commitment two factors, which promote empowerment.
- ***Number of Employees***–As their number increases, the functions of personnel management got enlarged and complex.
- ***Quality of Employees***–has also changed managing them need better appreciation of their exceptions and clear understanding of their psyche, feeling, attitude and sentiments. They should not be taken for granted.
- ***Sustainable Competitive Advantage***–In order to ensure that the employees are raised to the occasion they are to be highly both innovative and creative. The real challenge to the modern personnel managers is how to bring them to that level of enlightenment.
- ***The Greatest Challenge***–facing HRD managers is to find ways and means of empowering their employees.
- ***Social Orientation***– The modern personnel manager has 'social responsibility' and social responsiveness as two most important functions to perform.

- *Reservation Issues*–might be a challenge to merit in selection and promotion. Modern managers are exposed to such forces.
- *Personnel Managers*–will be under great strain to minimize manpower costs and at the same time acquire and retain talented employees at attractive compensation. The only alternative is to derive maximum efficiency and productivity from employees. This requires higher skills in personnel management so that interests of both the groups - employers and employees are attended to.
- *Future Challenges*–As time goes, some of the problems mentioned above may get solved, some may get acute, and a few new problems may arise (Nair N.G. and Nair Latha, 1999).

Expectations from HR Managers

The external forces relating to corporate reorganizations, global competition, declining market, changing work force demographics, employee expectations, and legal and governmental requirements represent long-term trends that have transformed the way organizations interact with employees. HR professionals are in a pivotal position in terms of these challenges.

HR professionals must look ahead with respect to corporate objectives - whether they involve a new line of business, a possible acquisition, or a new corporate emphasis and make sure that the HR policy is consistent with overall objectives. As the field of management began to mature, more emphasis began to be placed on the people manning the enterprise. Studies revealed that recognizing people for the work they had done influenced their productivity. Employees were becoming more demanding in what they wanted from their jobs. The vital nature of human resource management and its overall impact in modern organizations came to be recognized it with it, the influence of HR professionals began to increase by leaps and bounds.

Today a clear trend has emerged wherein a higher and higher proportion of HR directors either report to the very top of the management pyramid or become chief executives themselves. The HR professional in the coming decade must become more highly motivated, bottom line managers, completely in tune with the needs of the organizations top management. The trust is to be proactive - anticipating events, not just reacting to them - scanning the internal as well as external horizons, alerting management to the issues and problems likely to affect the organization and suggesting ways and means of addressing them (Chatterjee Bhaskar, 1995).

Future Roles for HR Work

HR practitioners of the future must demonstrate exemplary leadership skills if they are to be successful. They should be leaders who are capable of demonstrating a new value added component to their organization by managing and developing knowledge.

Key roles for HR leaders have emerged:

- As change agents, HR practitioners create and sustain progressive change.
- As HR, strategists, HR practitioners craft and implement long-term plans to gain competitive advantage through the HR function and through the organizations knowledge assets embodied by its people.
- When enacting the role of HR functional aligned, HR practitioners link their efforts to those of the organization and build consensus among the components of HR system.
- As partners to general managers, HR practitioners work closely with key line managers to ensure that the work environment is conducive to achieving high performance.
- As problem solvers and consultants, HR practitioners troubleshoot human performance problems and identify opportunities to avert those problems or to uncover and seize competitive advantage by unleashing the creative and talents of the organizations' people.

Future competencies needed by HR practitioners to be successful:

There are several types of HR competencies:

- *Leadership Oriented:* The following competencies are central to demonstrate HR leadership in future. (a) Credibility, (b) people skills, (c) understanding business, (d) consultative approach, (e) comfort with change and (f) developing credibility. True leaders combine their expertise of HR policies and practices with knowledge of the business to lead change effectively.
- *HR–management Oriented Competencies*–These competencies can be divided into two and will become increasingly important in the future. They were identified by Spencer and Spencer: a) for executives–strategic thinking, change leadership, relationship management, b) for managers–flexibility, empowering team facilitation, portability. These strategically oriented competencies fit well for any manager. However, they become increasingly more important for HR practitioners who accept the challenges of becoming fully involved and participating partner in the business, driving change in the organization and working to improve results for continuous improvement.
- *HR technically Oriented Competencies*– (a) level of competency currently available on the HR staff, (b) priority need for the competency to meet current and projected work load, (c) availability of the competency in the job market, (d) degree of competency customization needed to complement the organization culture of the customer being serviced.

They can be conceptualized in terms of a pyramid. A HR practitioner, whether a HR functional specialist or a generalist, can demonstrate any or all the competencies on the pyramid (William J. Rothwell, Robert K. Prescott, and Maria W. Taylor, 1999).

An Introduction to Human Resource Management

Human Resource Management is not something that can be left out to the professionals (that is to the HR manager). To be effective it must permeate the whole organization be owned by all managers and influence the attitudes, performance and motivation of all employees. It must operate in a number of ways in the organization and must be felt in all places. Significantly and unlike personnel management it needs to be integrated into the strategy level of organizations to be fully successful. So HRM is an activity for strategic managers, line managers and for HR professionals. Its applications can be seen in a number of areas:

- *Strategic Planning:* It is difficult to imagine that any business decision of any real significance can be taken without due reference to the human resource implications. Many decisions will have implications for training, staff deployment, manpower planning, and reward.
- *Planning human resources:* If·employees are central to the success of the organization, then how the actual and potential work force must develop in order to meet current and future challenges is of vital importance. The future demand for labours the supply of labour within the economy and the speed and methods by which labour will flow through the organization will need to be taken into account. This will involve HR managers working closely with colleagues in line management and with strategic planners.
- *Recruitment and selection:* Working with strategists and line managers, HR specialists will need to develop recruitment and selection policies and practices that are congruent with the wider and long-term aims of the organization. That is those employed now should not be employed with only the short term in mind. In times of rapid product obsolesce, changing and developing technologies and rewarding technical proficiency must be appropriate attitudes and a willingness to accept change as the normal state of being. The recruitment is for recruitment, selection policies that are both far-sighted owned, and implemented by line manages.
- *Reward Management:* HR managers will need to keep themselves apprised of reward systems new and emerging data and statistics concerning pay and its management and trends in conditions of service. Reward management

policies are not cast in stone and not only do they tend to corrupt overtime, they will also need fine-tuning and ultimately replacing as the objectives and the organization change (Beltom Trevor 2001).

Functions of Managers

The functions of managers provide a useful framework for organizing management knowledge.

Planning- Planning involves missions and objectives and the actions to achieve them, it requires decision making that is future courses of action among alternatives.

Organizing- People working together in groups to achieve some goal must have roles to play much like the actors fill in dramas, whether these roles are ones they develop themselves, are accidental or haphazard, or are defined and structured by someone who wants to make sure that people contribute in a specific way to group effort. The concept of a "role" implies that what people do has a definite purpose or objective they know how their objective fits into group effort and they have the necessary authority, tools and information to accomplish the task.

Staffing-Staffing involves filling and keeping filled positions in the organization structure. This is done by identifying workforce requirements, inventorying the people available; and recruiting selecting, placing, promoting, appraising, planning the careers of, compensating and training or otherwise developing both candidates and current jobholders to accomplish their tasks effectively and efficiently.

Leading- is the influencing of people so that they will contribute to organization and group goals, it has to do predominantly with the interpersonal aspect of managing. All managers would agree that their most important problems arise from people their desires and attitudes, their behaviour as individuals and in-groups, and that effective manager also need to be effective leaders.

Controlling-is the measuring and correcting of activities of subordinates to ensure that events conform to plans. It measures performance against goals and plans, shows where negative deviations exists and by putting in motion actions to correct deviations, helps ensure accomplishment of plans. Although planning must precede controlling, plans are not self-achieving. Plans guide managers in the use of resources to accomplish specific goals, and then activities are checked to determine whether they conform to the plans.

Co-ordination, the essence of managership: Some authorities consider coordination to be a separate function of the manager. It seems more accurate, however to regard it as the essence of managership for achieving harmony among individual efforts toward the accomplishment of group goals. Each of the managerial functions is an exercise contributing coordination (Koontz Harold and Weihrich Heinz, 1998).

Essentials of Organizational Behaviour

HR managers need to recognize that their employees react to perceptions, not to reality. So whether managers' appraisal, of an employee is actually objective and unbiased or whether the organizations' levels are actually among the highest in the industry is less relevant than what employees perceive. Individuals who perceive appraisals as biased or wage levels as low will have as if those conditions actually exist. Employees naturally organize and interpret what they see; inherent in this process is the potential or perceptual distortion.

The message to managers should be clear. They need to pay close attention to how employees perceive both their jobs and management practices.

- **Learning–** The issue is not whether employees continually learn on the job or not. They do! The only issue is whether they are going to manage learning through the rewards they allocate and the examples they set. If marginal employees are rewarded with pay raises and promotions they will have little reason to change their behaviour. If managers want behaviour A and rewarded B, it shouldn't surprise them to find employees learning to engage in behaviour B. Similarly managers should expect that employees will look to them as models. Managers who are constantly late to work or take 2 hours for lunch or help them to company office supplies for personal uses should expect employees to read the message they're sending and model their behaviour accordingly.

- **Attitudes–** Managers should be interested in their employee's attitudes because attitudes influence behaviour. Satisfied employees for instance have lower rates of turnover and absenteeism than dissatisfied employees do. Given that managers want to keep resignations and absenteeism down, especially among the more productive employees. They will want to do those things that will generate positive job attitudes.

The findings about the satisfaction-productivity relation have important implications for managers. They suggest that the goal of making employees happy on the assumption that doing so will lead to high productivity be probably misdirected. Managers would get better results by directing there employees primarily to what will help employees become more productive. Successful job performance should then lead to feelings of accomplishment, increased pay, promotions and other rewards—all outcomes-which then lead to satisfaction with the job.

Managers should also be aware, that employees would try to reduce cognitive dissonance. More important dissonance can be managed. If employees are required to engage in activities that appear inconsistent to them or that are at odds with their attitudes the pressures to reduce the resulting dissonance can be lessened when the employee perceive the dissonance as externally or of the rewards are significant enough to offset the dissonance (Robbins Stephen, 2000).

Management of Organization Behaviour

When followers are at low levels of readiness, the manager must take the responsibility for the traditional management functions such as planning, organizing, motivating, and controlling. The manager's role is that of motivating and controlling. However, when managers develop their people and have followers at high levels of readiness, the followers can take over much of the responsibility for this day to day traditional management functions. The manager's role can then change from supervisor to the group's representative in the next level of the organization. If they develop followers who can take responsibility for their own tasks on a day to day basis managers can invest their time in their high "pay-off" management functions, the "linking-pin" activities that enhance the group's performance. These functions include acquiring resources necessary for maximizing the group's productivity communicating horizontally and vertically and co-ordinations the group's efforts with those of other departments to improve overall productivity.

The manager instead of getting trapped in problems has time for long-range strategic planning and creativity.

Initially close supervision and direction are helpful when working with individuals who have little experience in directing their own behaviour. The manager recognizes that this style is only a first step. In order to maximize their potential in the high pay-off functions, managers must change their style and take an active role in helping other grow. The development of followers depends not only on the managers' behaviour but also on values and expectations.

The first question managers have to ask when they are thinking about developing their people is; what area of my employees' work do I want to influence? In other words, what are their responsibilities or goals and objectives? A foreman, e.g., might want to influence productivity quality, waste, absenteeism, accident rate, and so on. Once the objectives or responsibilities are identified and understood, managers must clearly specify what constitutes good performance in approaching the desired level. What does a good sales record mean? Does it mean a certain number of sale made or dollar volume of sales? What is meant by 'developing your people' or 'being good administrator?' managers have to specify what good performance looks like. Just telling a person 'I want you to make 200 widgets a day for managers and staff members to know well someone is doing good performance has to be clearly specified. Managers can not change and develop their follower's behaviour in areas that are unclear (Hersey and Blanchard, 2001).

HR is a Co-operative and Strategic Activity

According to Molander and Winterton, human resource management is a co-operative, strategic and hardheaded activity staffed by managers committed to the overall success of the organization.

Following are the areas where HR professionals are involved and play important roles—

- **Strategic Planning-** HR professionals are involved in the overall and to coherent long term planning and shorter term management, control and monitoring of an organization's human resources so as to gain from them maximum added value and to best position them to achieve the organization's corporate goals and mission.
- **Recruitment and Selection-**Working with strategists and line managers, HR specialists will need to develop recruitment and selection policies and practices that are congruent with the wider and long-term aims of the organization.
- **Reward Management-**HR managers need to keep themselves apprised of reward systems new and emerging, data and statistics concerning pay and its conditions of services.
- **Training-** The use of development and use of analytical appraisal methods as well as the undertaking of regular reviews of departmental progress, performance and challenges should allow the line managers to identify the training needs of the employees. The HR specialists have input into form and framework within which this training needs identification takes place and contributes to the

formulation of the corporate training plan (Beltom Trevor, 2001).

Stresses and Health Problems of Metro Managers

Managers' health is important for healthy development of the organizations, as they govern the institutions at various levels. Hence, it is important to currently review the stresses, health problems, and coping behaviours of the managers. This paper throws light upon the most common workplace stresses and challenges, the most commonly experienced health problems among the managers.

Indian managers have been studied by researchers on multiple issues that matter to them in the organizations for developing insightful understanding and building better future perspective in the Indian industry. The 26 issues that emerged from 72 current research studies have been submerged into psychological, professional and social/organizational factors as below:

Psychological	*Professional*	*Social/Organizational*
Managers' Stress and Related Aspects	Attitude towards Profession	Manager's Power and Political Activities at Work
Job Involvement	Difference Between Male and Female Managers	Work Ethics
Values	Women Managers	Managerial Turnover
Need Satisfaction	Managerial Effectiveness	Organizational Communication
Cognitive Styles of Indian Managers	Managing People at Work	Organizational Effectiveness
Managerial Job Satisfaction	Managerial Styles	Managerial Roles
Executive's self esteem	Time Management	Managerial Promotions
Achievement Motivation among Managers	Human Resource Management	Organizational Systems
	Strategy Implementation	Managerial Attitudes towards Unions

The issues that have not got attention of the Indian researchers, but are very much prevalent in the organizational practice are: Total Quality Management (TQM), Standards (ISO series), family-run business, and the managerial health.

In order to enrich the managerial health perspective in the Indian context, this article describes the major stresses and challenges at the workplace of the Indian managers, and their health problems due to work pressures. It also deals with the managers' coping with stresses and challenges, based on a study of 120 managers in 2002. Of which, 86 were male (72 per cent) and 34 female (28 per cent) managers in Mumbai with 97 per cent having age between 24 to 40 years and the rest above 41. The 94 per cent had work experience between 3 to 10 years and the rest above 21 year (Kaila H. L. 2003).

HRD Practices in Indian Industries

Human Resource Development (HRD) is a process by which employees of an organization acquire and develop their capabilities and inner-potentials continuously to perform various functions or roles assigned to them by the organization. It ensures development of their "self" and the "organization." Thus, HR professionals aim at helping employees to acquire competencies through HRD, potential appraisal organizational development (OD), role analysis, goal-setting, career-planning, training and development, etc.

Pareek and Rao identified the following objectives of HRD systems and practices:

(a) Provide a comprehensive framework and methods for the development of human resources in an organization.

(b) Generate systematic information about human resources for purposes of manpower planning, placement, succession, planning, and the like.

(c) Increase the capabilities of an organization to recruit, retain, and motivate talented employees.

(d) Create a climate that enables every employee to discover, develop, and use his/her capabilities to a fuller extent in order to further both individual and organizational goals.

Thus, it is now evident that HRD is not just a theoretical concept, it is a practical and dynamic concept and is being practiced in various organizations in India. (Jain V.K. 1996).

HRD and Organizational Effectiveness

According to T.V. Rao, there exist an inter-relationship between HRD instruments, processes; outcomes and organizational effectiveness. Following can be postulated about the linkages between HRD mechanisms and processes:—

- HRD departments and mechanisms are useful instruments for initiating and strengthening development processes and culture and achieving HRD outcomes.
- HRD mechanisms and subsystems should be designed keeping in view the HRD process and culture to be achieved.
- Irrespective of how well the mechanisms are designed and implemented, if the top management does not have commitment to HRD and communicate such commitment to all employees, the HRD mechanisms may become more rituals in wastage of managerial time rather than leading to the development of HRD processes.

In a view of these the HRD managers have complex role to perform. In order to make an impact, the HRD manager should

- Have a high degree of perseverance,
- Have a high degree of commitment to HRD and HRD philosophy;
- Be closer to the chief executive and be able to get and communicate the top–management's commitment to employees; and
- Be given enough time to work as HRD manager without being transferred (Joseph Jerome and Singh Kuldeep, 1998).

HR Challenges in the Coming Decades

In the present years HRD professionals are called upon to deal with the problems of people who are affected by the fall-out of globalization process. The people affected can be classified into two broad groups those already in employment and in future. In respect of those already in employment HR, professionals have the responsibility to train them to develop competencies in the organization in which they work. In the process, they will have to wean them away from the influence of unions and remove suspicion if any, from their minds which they may have towards the employers and develop a sense of trust and commitment to the organization, as its goals.

This task is not easy to accomplish. As facilitators of change in organization they are also called upon to deal with problems resulting from restructuring measures adopted by the organization. The success of such plans can be assured if the HR managers manage to create and maintain an image of trust and awareness among the employees and succeed in persuading them to accept the changes as basic need for organizational effectiveness and survival (Rao A.K. 1998-99).

HR Pioneers Explore the Road Less Travelled

As leaders and planners of global human resource strategy, HR professionals were attired to their unique challenges and opportunities as business continues to forge new markets in a world increasingly without borders. HR leaders from around the world converge at conference to share problems, information, stories and advice on topics ranging from how to deal global staffing issues, to getting international compensation policies right. They talked about how cultural differences influence, how you conduct business. They debated global health care issues. They discussed worldwide problems. They considered expatriate relocation mistakes. They pondered overseas legal minefields. They shared employee repatriation stories. They commiserated over designing global HRMS system. The sympathized over assessing performance in a worldwide setting. In a word they brain stormed.

It was a 3-day think tank for global HR leadership. These themes emerged to guide them into the year 2000 and beyond. Business is becoming more global and HR needs to be at the centre of making it happen. Companies need to adopt their practices to other part of the world, rather than just transplanting American ways. And finally, HR needs to develop a more complete way to recruit and manage global workers so that individual career path reflect global empties and responsibilities and meld from the start with long-term global business strategy.

It's a tough job. But HR professionals can and must do it. The future of business depends on it (Laabs Jennifer J. 1996).

Changing Concept in Corporate Government and HRM Outlook

HRM is a distinct wing of professional managers. Democratization of institutions at all levels has placed enormous powers in the hands of ordinary people. The current scenario is full of uncertainties and under perception. Vacating the turbulent caldron of emerging ideas, rising aspirations and raving conflicts, the HR manager is often confused not knowing which path he may choose in the junction where he is at present standing.

HRD is no longer confined to mere training and development of employees. It is necessary for HR managers to look beyond his organization. His duty does not stop at recruitment from the available manpower resource. He may have to go out expertise in the society to achieve results. Similarly, his responsibility may not be over as soon as the retires and his dues are paid. Post employment settlement and continuing relationship for utilization of the experience and skills of retiring employee may become necessary for mutual advantage. The task of HR managers thus would be ennoblement of people through all round development (George Kuriyan, 1999-2000).

Psychological Job Strain and Productivity in Human Service Workers

The aim of the study was to test the main and interactive effects of the key dimensions of the demand-control-support model in psychology, predicting levels of strain (specifically emotional exhaustion, depersonalization and job dissatisfaction) and feeling of productivity and competency (personal accomplishment) in a multi-occupational sample of human service workers.

Controlling for demographics, negative affectivity (NA) and quadratic terms structural equation analysis showed some support for the additive strain hypothesis: jobs combining high demands, low control and low support produced the lowest levels of satisfaction in workers. High demands and low support only were associated with high depersonalization and high emotional exhaustion.

Support was also found for the additive active learning hypotheses: jobs combining high demands and high control produced the highest levels of personal accomplishment. The study supports job redesign interventions for improving, workers, well being and productivity (Swanson V., Judith P. Walker and R.J. Simpson, 2000).

Work-strain Relationship in Thirteen Occupations

Much of the researches on the work-strain relationship utilize models which are narrowly focused in only a few job characteristics. These models are often global in their approach, failing to account for specific situations. Addressing these two issues, the present study investigated the influence of seven job characteristics namely work control and six sources of work pressure across a range of thirteen occupations, on mental and physical ill-health.

The six sources of work pressure were factors in the job, organizational role, relationships at work, career development, organizational climate and home/work pressures. The occupations were – civil servants, government workers group 1 and 2, Air traffic controllers, Anesthetics, manual workers, physicians, administrative health workers, paramedics, nursing staff, telecommunication engineers and accountants.

The aim of the study was to clarify the extent to which a range of different job factors can influence health and well being.

The results indicated differences in mean scores for the study variables in 13 occupations. Compared with all the workers, the group 1 government workers had relatively low mean scores for seemed to have better mental and health then other occupations with their low mental and physical ill health scores. Thus their employees may have good work environment with supportive leadership, good career structure and social relations. Air traffic controllers perceived the highest amount of work controls. Mean scores physicians, pharmacists and nursing staffs were high on organizational role source of pressure. In the present economic climate of public sectors cut backs many physicians have to switch between the role of managing staff and budgets and patients care.

The pooled within group correlation for both mental and physical ill health indicated that all of the 7 job characteristics in the present study are indeed important. Work control and the six sources of pressures as measured by the OSI were all significantly related to ill health (Sparks Kate and Cary L. Coopers, 1999).

Organizational Behaviour and HRM

This book reflects upon the significant issues of HR and OB ranging from recruitment to international HRM. This presentation of 14 chapters is based on comprehensive literature review and empirical evidences with case studies and illustrations from the Indian industries.

The aim of this publication is to present the current researched knowledge on crucial HR issues such as recruitment, performance appraisal, communication, decision making, group processes, job satisfaction, leadership, organizational development interventions, training effectiveness, organizational culture, women managers, mentoring and coaching, HRM in NGOs, and international human resource management.

Chapter 1 'organizational culture' while defining organization culture elaborates on the concept of work culture.

It describes how organizational culture develops and throws light on assessing an organization's culture.

Chapter 2 'women managers' describes current research studies on women managers, and female secretaries to managers in organizations.

Chapter 3 'mentoring and coaching' explains that coaching and mentoring are not the same things. The results and experience support that mentoring is a power free, two-way mutually beneficial learning situation where the mentor provides advice, shares knowledge, and experiences, and teaches self-discovery approach. The chapter highlights the coach mentor distinction, the coaching and mentoring processes, barriers to coaching and mentoring, mentoring and women, importance of coaching and mentoring, mentoring programs and its benefits.

Voluntary organizations work with and very often on behalf of others. NGO cover a wide spectrum from small local organization to nation wide federations and international network. The issues they tackle might be anything from the human rights to the entire mosaic of development concerns. In India, individual states have networks of NGO. Over the last decade, there has been a high increase in the number of NGO. According to the Economist (1999), the number of international NGO has risen to more than 26000 from 6000 in 1990. Chapter 4 describes the role of 'HRM in NGOs'.

Chapter 5 explains the 'international human resource management' by ways of expatriate selection, cultural requirements, expatriate training, developing international staff and multinational teams, objectives of international compensation, international human resource management approach, and management in international perspective.

Chapter 6 'recruitment' raises question on what channels did the recruiter use to make hires. A hiring procedure works best on a foundation provided by job analysis, labour budgeting, and skillful recruitment.

Performance appraisal serves many purposes explains Chapter 7 on 'performance appraisal'. It details about the performance evaluation, purposes of performance evaluation, performance evaluation system, rating scales and methods of performance evaluation.

Many studies have pointed out to the areas where communication is vital to the success of an organization. Managers in organizations are eager to improve communication in order to achieve widespread acceptance of standards and values necessary for the survival and success of their enterprise. Chapter 8 on 'organizational communication' describes the communication process.

Chapter 9 on 'decision making' defines good and bad decisions, behavioural decision theory, organizational decision theory, managers and decision-making, formal intuitive decision-making.

Chapter 10 'group processes' describes the group behaviour, formation, and development of work groups, group-think, the group cohesiveness, group-shift, inter-group conflict, group decision-making, group decision-making techniques, nominal group technique.

Chapter 11 'job satisfaction' explains the nature of job satisfaction, reasons for job satisfaction, factors that influences job satisfaction, theories of job satisfaction, techniques for measuring job satisfaction, principle causes of job satisfaction, and how to reduce job satisfaction.

Leadership is the catalyst that transforms potential into reality. Leadership is the process of influencing and supporting others to work enthusiastically toward achieving objectives. Chapter 12 explains 'leadership in organizational goals'.

Chapter13 'organizational development interventions' emphasis on changing the organizational culture, resistance to change and overcoming organizational resistance to change. Every organization needs to have well-trained and experienced people to perform the activities that have to be done. It is necessary to raise the skill levels and increase the versatility and adaptability of the employees. This is done through training.

Chapter14 'training effectiveness' explains why evaluate, what to evaluate, how to evaluate, follow up, levels of evaluation, method to isolate the effects of training (Kaila H.L. 2003).

Psychological Profile of Female Executive

This study examined various issues related to occupational life of female managers. These included satisfaction with occupational life, various reasons to work, and fulfillment of job expectations. Anxiety/stress in case of job expectations not fulfilled attributes to success etc. The data obtained showed that significant number of women executives (64.2 per cent) feel that some expectations regarding their job are fulfilled. 68.66 per cent of them feel that if their job expectations are not fulfilled it leads to stress manifested in forms like irritability, hypertension, depression, and in many other ways. The author also discussed various gender equity issues influencing women executives. These included:

- Whether male executives are evaluated on the same basis as female executives.
- Whether female executives has been seen as unfeminine because she exerted her authority.
- Whether a female executive feels that working in the set-up, that she is in is breaking its a man's world and many such others issues.

Women executives feel that their male counterparts are evaluated on the same basis as they are, also female executives feel that they have been seen as unfeminine because they exerted their authority and that they do not feel that working in the set-up that they are in, is breaking into man's world (Kaila H.L.1997).

Summary

The major conclusions that have emerged from the 105 HR researches are:

- **The functions and qualifications of HR managers differ** from one organization to another. They have to be sensitive towards human values and problems, needs of employees, and the concerns of the organization. Moreover, human resource professionals have special role to play in managing change in the organization. The HR professionals are contributing to an overall customer relationship management strategy.

- **A new role of the human resources professionals** is emerging. The new role of the HR manager must be parallel to the needs of his changing organization. The HR manager must play an integral role in the organizational success. Manager's roles are mainly decisional, interpersonal, and informational for effective role-playing.
- **HR professionals have gained focus and importance** as companies systemize the functions of human resources management. They are gaining credibility in the organizations. HR functions have also gained prominence in business decisions.
- **The impact of human resource management** has provided the HR directors a great deal of influence in today's enterprise. The senior management is recognizing the importance of the human resources department.
- **Managing a group of heterogeneous people** throw a formidable task to modern managers. Managerial leadership skills are the buzzword. The quality of communication skill is something that the HR manager must have.
- **The greatest challenge facing HR managers** is to find ways of empowering the employees. The major concern of HRD is achieving and maintaining a satisfied workforce.
- **The HR managers need to be knowledgeable about business trends** and issues. They need to look for newer and effective approaches to improving organizational performance.
- **Stress is a major concern of HRM.** A goal of HR specialists is to equip employees to manage their stress. They have to constantly plan strategies to achieve better health of their employees.
- **HR managers must be in regular touch with the key line managers** and staff. They need to develop systems such as

performance feedback, potential promotion, career planning and development, and internal networking.

- **The ultimate goal of HR managers** is to achieve the learning and self-sustaining organization. The proactive and business oriented human resource managers have to become the catalysts of change. The dynamic HR managers build progressive organizations.
- **Without the integrated human resource policies and strategies**, organizations are less likely to survive. The human resource managers play an increasingly significant role, as the organizations take diversity initiatives.
- **The organizations also need to take steps** to ensure both the physical and mental health of HR managers so that they can contribute towards the development of the healthy organizations and a better business environment.

2
The Psychological Constructs of Managers

A survey on managers' personality type, learning and leadership styles found that most managers are A - personality type, used an abstract conceptualization learning style, and preferred a transactional style of leadership. This chapter provides a detailed account of these psychological constructs of Indian managers.

Introduction

The managers in organizations administer the entire business and commerce. This is the segment of our society that can put us either on a marvelous progress path or lead the organization to only an average performance. Managers govern our institutions and its business. Hence it is important to understand the psychology of our managers? What kind of personality predisposition they have?

What are their learning styles, and more importantly what are their predominant leadership styles? There may also be possible interactions between these psychological dimensions of managers that drive them to behave, perform and achieve inadequately or greatly. There may also be possible gender as well as cultural differences on these managerial variables.

With these psychological background constructs in mind, one tends to believe that each manager in an organization will have a particular personality type, learning and leadership style.

He or she is definitely a unique person with different styles of these characteristics. Of course in selection of a manager, these cognitive, behavioural and personality factors are important. But in an organization there might be a group of managers with differences in their personality type, learning as well as leadership styles. To handle these internal differences in the managerial profile may be a difficult task until the organizations are aware of these differences, and sufficient steps are being taken to bring these psychological differences into regular interactions for developing mutual understanding. These differences in psychological constructs of the managers can prove to be either beneficial or harmful to the organization. Beneficial in the sense if they are positively regarded as unique individual potentials and utilized; harmful in the sense if they are not considered or ignored in group interactions and teamwork which may lead to conflicts. Hence it is very important to understand the psychological constructs of managers in an organization in terms of their personality type, learning as well as leadership styles. With these questions in mind, the researcher carried out the present study in Mumbai.

Indian managers have been studied by researchers on multiple issues that matter to them in the organizations for developing insightful understanding and building better future perspective in the Indian industry. The managerial research studies have examined several psychological, professional and social, organizational factors (Kaila, 2002, 2003).

Researches on Personality Type

Based on 20 years of psychological research, Farley Frank (1990) came up with a common cluster of characteristics that make up the "Type T Personality." The T stands for Thrill Seekers. These high profile people are risk takers and adventurous who seek excitement and stimulation wherever they can find or create it. He also researched on some Thrill Seekers, who have Outstanding Creativity (T Plus), but it can lead others to be extremely Destructive, even criminal behaviour, they seek stimulation and thrill on the dark side of the street (T Minus). He segregated the T personality into constructive and destructive further subdividing them into mental and physical.

The Type T Personality is most often found among those in the 16-24 ranges. Research compared people of different ages, so it is believed that most people reach their strongest expression of Type T in their late teens to early 20s, with a decline into old age (Farley, 1990). People who demand thrilling experiences in their lives can turn out to be creative and adventurous or antisocial and criminal depending on the outlets available to them.

Salgado (1997) statistically combined results conducted through Meta analysis of 36 European studies success in the United States, Canada, and Europe and found that personality traits predict employee success. He concluded that personality factors in Europe operate largely as they do in the United States and Canada. The following was found:

Conscientiousness and emotional stability are valid for all occupations and for all criteria (supervisory ratings, training success, and history as tracked by personnel records such as promotions and the like). Conscientiousness is the most predictive of employee performance over all other factors. Extraversion predicts the performance of managers and police. Openness is a valid predictor for police and skilled labour jobs. Agreeableness shows the lowest relationship to employee success, a correlation of almost zero. Agreeableness was associated with training success. Openness is a valid predictor of training success. All personality trait relationships with employee job success or training are small. Therefore, they are not the total pictures by a long shoot.

However, as the U.S. and Canada have similar culture and value systems, for purposes of business, and also similar approaches to employee selection and evaluation the researcher, Jesus Salgado of University of Santiago de Compostela in Spain, wondered if these factors were also predictors in other parts of the world.

Pestonjee (2001) investigated the moderating effect of Type-A pattern of behaviour disposition on the relationship between role stresses and state-trait anger. It was argued that human personality and certain forms of stresses and closely related and theorized that Type-A individuals high concern for control over environment and maladaptive coping behaviours decrease their ability to tolerate stresses and, consequently, manifestations of stress such as anger increase. In the light of the findings of this study, the authors made several suggestions. First, a more careful selection and placement of Type-A individuals is needed at the time of job assignment. Second, a systematic programme of educating Type-A individuals about the personal and health dangers they may encounter in the work environment may prove useful. Finally, a regular audits of Type-A employees health may be necessary to detect early symptoms of physical and mental health problems.

A good match between individual personality and organization is essential. Mismatch between personality and organization structure may lead to stress, confusion and chaos, loss of interest by members in the organization, low morale and job satisfaction.

Researches on Learning Styles

Ahmad and Varghese (1991) attempted to validate aspects of Kolb's Experiental Learning Theory in the Indian context as well as examine the relationship between learning style mismatch and job satisfaction. The sample consisted of 103 management students and 68 practicing managers. The results point to some interesting findings regarding the learning style in Indian Management Professionals. Indian Managers were found to be more oriented towards the concrete and active ends of the abstract/abstract and the active/reflective dimensions as compared to Kolb's sample of their western counterparts. It was found that the people dominated the functional areas within the field of management with the particular style profile demanded by the area. Finally a significant relationship emerged between a match of learning style with the work area and job satisfaction.

The National Centre for Vocational Education Research Ltd. (NCVER) conducted a recent research that aimed to identify training and learning practices that demonstrated positive benefits over a period of time. It primarily focused on the integration of teaching and learning within the firm, factors that influence firms to recruit existing skills as opposed to developing skills sets within the firm, the use of accredited training and training packages, the development of career structures within firms, the impact of globalization on training and learning practices, and returns on their investment in training.

The research concluded that most organizations had a cultures in which there was respect for all individuals, a willingness to share knowledge and expertise, and a positive attitude or 'can do' mentality among workers, was essential to successful training and learning. 'Open communication' and, in particular, cross-functional team consultations, also stimulated learning, which led to innovative solutions. A supportive learning culture also encouraged individual development through its human resource practices, such as providing training and learning opportunities for all workers, career planning and promoting opportunities within the organization, and individual performance feedback in a performance management system. Within such a culture, employee achievements were recognized through employee or team awards for excellence, quality and consistency or goal-orientated bonus reward schemes. In addition, having a graded competency system ensured that excellence in performance was recognized (Susan Dawe, 2002)

Researches on Leadership Styles

Burns (1978) defined transactional leadership as occurring when one person takes the initiative in reaching others to exchange valued things. The purposes of leader and follower could be separate but are related, at least insofar as the purposes stand within the exchange process and can be advanced by maintaining that process or transaction.

Does the Transactional-Transformational Leadership Paradigm Transcend Organizational and National Boundaries? Bass (1997) found out that there is universality in the transactional-transformational leadership paradigm. Evidence supporting the paradigm has been gathered from all continents except Antarctica—even offshore in the North Sea. That is the same conception of phenomena and relationships can be observed in a wide range of organizations and cultures. Three corollaries are discussed. Supportive evidence has been gathered in studies conducted in organizations in business, education, the military, the government and the independent sector. The paradigm is sufficiently broad to provide a basis for measurement and understanding that is as universal as the concept of leadership itself. Exceptions can be understood as a consequence of unusual attributes of the organizations or cultures. Likewise supportive evidence has been accumulated from all but the one continent to document the applicability of the paradigm.

Sarros and Santora (2001) explored the nature of transformational and transactional leadership among business executives. Initially 181 executives were surveyed using the Multi-factor Leadership Questionnaire (MLQ), and subsequently 35 of the executives provided additional commentary both written and verbal. Results reveal that most executives believe there are weaknesses as well as strengths with both leadership constructs in practice. Overall, major leadership strengths are in the role modeling, coaching, and consideration behaviours of executives. Major weaknesses are in failure to motivate and challenge workers beyond the expected outcomes. Other facets of each of the four transformational and two transactional leadership behaviours are examined in this article. Lists leadership strategies and approaches for achieving positive results and implications for future research are also provided.

Manning (2002) investigated how gender and organizational level interact to influence ratings of leadership and work satisfaction, and argues that transformational leadership permits women to simultaneously carry out leadership and gender roles. Findings of a study of the management team of a large US social services agency confirmed predicted similarities in male and female managers' transformational leadership and work satisfaction. Top managers of both sexes saw themselves as more transformational leaders, while their raters perceived them as less transformational than average for the sample. Those who were younger and at lower managerial levels were more likely to underrate themselves as leaders, while their raters viewed them as higher than average in transformational leadership. The results are discussed in terms of how organizational status, experiences and feedback processes influence individuals' leadership perceptions and the potential obstacles to women's accurate assessment of their leadership abilities.

Khurana's (2002) findings are based on a study of the hiring and firing of CEOs at over 850 of America's largest companies and on extensive interviews with CEOs, corporate board members, and consultants at executive search firms.

His research explains the basic mechanics of the selection process of CEO's and how hiring priorities have changed with the rise of shareholder activism. Charisma—a quality once associated with religious and political leadership—has become the primary qualification for the CEO's job. Where charisma is the main criterion of employment, qualified candidates are extraordinarily scarce. Industry wisdom, company relationships, and technological expertise are all matter in our new knowledge-based enterprises. His research emphasis on charisma that artificially limits the number of candidates considered, giving them extraordinary leverage to demand high salaries and power. It also raises expectations and increases the chance that a CEO will be fired for failing to meet shareholders' hopes. The result is corporate instability and too little attention to long-term strategy. "Companies reflexively look to charismatic CEOs to save them, and that's a bad idea" according to Khurana.

How do leadership ratings collected from units operating under stable conditions predict subsequent performance of those units operating under high stress and uncertainty? To examine this question, the authors calculated the predictive relationships for the transformational and transactional leadership of 72 light infantry rifle platoon leaders for ratings of unit potency, cohesion, and performance for U.S. Army platoons participating in combat simulation exercises. Both transformational and transactional contingent reward leadership ratings of platoon leaders and sergeants positively predicted unit performance. The relationship of platoon leadership to performance was partially mediated through the unit's level of potency and cohesion. Implications, limitations, and future directions for leadership research are discussed (Bass et al, 2003).

Sample: 10 Managers both males and females at middle as well as senior levels from 12 organizations were selected. The total of 120 managers between the age range of 30 to 54 had enriching years of experience. Most of the managers had their education upto post-graduation. The types of organizations participated in the study were hotels, hospitals, banks, airlines, finance, computers, shipping, engineering, chemical, consultancy, etc. The managers represented different departments such as sales, marketing, labouratory, maintenance, human resources etc of their respective organizations.

Tools: Three questionnaires were used as mentioned below:

One was the Prabhu's Stress Profile, to measure Personality type. This section had 10 questions. The managers had to give ratings on the frequency of the occurrence of these situations in their day-to-day life on a 5-point scale

The next tool was a Leadership Questionnaire. Here, Managers had to distribute 5 points each for 20 statements, A and B types in order of the frequency of their occurrences. Scoring for these was on the basis of the ratings for each statement. The results would indicate the type of leadership qualities the managers possessed, i.e., Transformational Leadership / Transactional Leadership.

The third tool was The Learning Style Inventory. Here 36 different learning styles / characteristics were listed and managers had to rate which styles they used most often. The words were equally distributed in sets of fours resulting in 9 sets. Managers had to distribute 4 points in an ascending order depicting their most used learning styles. Scoring was calculated on the basis of addition of points listed for selected sets of questions, which fell under the four processes of Concrete Experience, Reflective Observation, Abstract Conceptualization and Active Experimentation (Kolb, 1984, 1997).

The last part of the tools was a questionnaire with an additional section for managers to describe their experiences in various organizations and what they learnt from them. Also, the Managers designation, years of experience, educational qualifications was a requirement.

Procedure: The questionnaires were given individually to each manager. The managers were acquainted with the instructions listed down on each questionnaire. Clarifications regarding any questions were provided. It took them roughly 30 minutes to complete all the questionnaires. The cooperation was to the fullest and all the questions were answered appropriately and openly. The managers were thanked for taking out time from their busy schedule and complying the study requirements.

Operational Definitions

Personality: Personality is the conglomeration of personal beliefs, expectations, desires, values, and behaviours that derive from the interaction between culture and the individual. Personality is the behaviours and techniques for solving problems that are used by an individual. Personality is to the individual as culture is to the group. The stable set of individual characteristics that makes us unique.

Type A Personality: A theory used to describe a person with a significant number of traits focused on urgency, impatience, success, and excessive competition. Hardworking, ambitious, and aggressive personality traditionally thought to be at greater risk for heart disease than other personality types. Contemporary studies show that having a Type A personality is only a risk factor for heart disease in regard to certain Type A characteristics, include frequent anger, chronic hostility, or inherent cynicism.

Type B Personality: The type B personality is relaxed, un-competitive, and inclined to self-analysis. Type B is characterized by a relaxed, deliberate, patient, and non-competitive approach to life with little need for advancement and achievement.

Leadership: Leadership is the art of creating an environment and influencing people to willingly follow a chosen direction. It requires clear vision and guides followers along a path that realizes the vision. It is the process of persuading, inspiring, motivating and influencing others.

Transformational Leadership: Transformational leadership involves the empowerment of employees, individualized consideration for subordinates and support for their ideas (Bass, 1997). Transformational leaders enable employees to influence outcomes of decisions that affect them. Beyond that, transformational leaders motivate their followers to be participants in an equitable relationship. Transformational leaders engage in activities that promote identification-based trust.

Transactional Leadership: Transactional leaders guide or motivate individual contributors in the direction of established goals by clarifying role and task requirements. The mechanisms of transactional leadership range from controlling ideas such as values, goals and specific objectives to more concrete systems defined by policy, process, and procedure.

Learning: The process by which relatively permanent changes occur in behavioural potential as a result of experience is learning. Reflecting on experience to identify how a situation or future actions could be improved and then using this knowledge to make actual improvements. This can be individual or group-based. Learning involves applying lessons learned to future actions, which provides the basis for another cycle of learning.

Concrete Experience (CE): This means involving oneself fully, openly, without bias in new experiences. Learning from specific experiences, relating to people, sensitivity to feelings. It is identifying what factors have led people to experience frustration and dissatisfaction and further articulating these factors.

Reflective Observation (RO): It is carefully observing before making judgment, viewing from different perspectives, looking for meaning. The questions that usually come in one's mind when using these styles are what might we do about these factors. Why the frustration and dissatisfaction? Are they essential components of the programming process? What alternative approaches to programming would ameliorate or even eliminate them?

Abstract Conceptualization (AC): Here, one Creates concepts and generalizations to integrate and make sense of the experience, the reflections and the observations, develop theories. It is learning by thinking. One uses logical analysis of ideas, systematic planning, and acts on intellectual understanding.

Active Experimentation (AE): It is the ability to get things done, by taking risks and by influence people and events through action. Here they test implications of concepts in new situations - use theories to make decisions and solve problems. It is learning by doing. The questions bouncing in minds of people with such a learning style are let's build some programs! Try out our ideas!

Personality Type, Leadership, and Learning Styles of Managers

Table 1 below is a group data table of 120 managers on dimensions of personality. Here, firstly we look at the personality dimension. Taking a close look at the personality types, we observe that 55 per cent of managers have type A - personality type, people under this category are hardworking, ambitious and energetic. One out of every five managers (20 per cent) fell under Type A personality, this often result in stress, heart ailments, and other coronary diseases. Type A's usually have high levels of competitiveness, ambition, workaholic attitude, irritable, restless with other's pace, reluctant to share power, over committed guilt over relaxing always works more than eight hours a day.

The 22 per cent managers were B+ personality type. People with Type B personality are relaxed and un-competitive. They have a take it easy attitude in life. They take life as it comes.

Table 1

Personality Type (N=120)

Organization No.	*Type B*	*Type B+*	*Type A-*	*Type A*	*Type A+*
			Personality Types		
1.	-	-	9	1	-
2.	-	4	6	-	-
3.	-	1	9	-	-
4.	3	-	7	-	-
5.	3	-	-	7	-
6.	-	1	7	2	-
7.	-	4	5	1	-
8.	-	-	-	10	-
9.	-	6	4	-	-
10.	2	4	2	2	-
11.	-	2	8	-	-
12.	1	-	8	1	-
Total	**9 (7%)**	**22(18%)**	**65 (55%)**	**24 (20%)**	**0**

Table 2 below is a group data on leadership styles of transactional and transformational leadership on 120 managers.

Mumbai mangers have shown transactional leadership style (65 per cent). These leaders motivate employees to achieve prescribed goals. Transactional leaders prefer controlling ideas such as values, goals and specific objectives to more concrete systems defined by policy, process, and procedure.

The remaining 35 per cent managers indicate transformational leadership style. Transformational leaders enable employees to influence outcomes of decisions that affect them. Beyond that, transformational leaders motivate their followers to be participants in an equitable relationship. They trust their employees and have full faith that their employees won't let them down. They don't like to impose too much control on their subordinates.

Table 2

Leadership Styles (N= 120)

Organization No.	**Leadership Styles** *Transactional*	*Transformational*
1.	10	-
2.	9	1
3.	5	5
4.	5	5
5.	4	6
6.	8	2
7.	-10	-
8.	4	6
9.	5	5
10.	6	4
11.	6	4
12.	6	4
Total	**78 (65%)**	**42 (35%)**

Table 3 below is a group data table indicating the different learning styles at managerial level through the four processes of abstract conceptualization, active experimentation, concrete experience, and reflective observation.

The 35 per cent of managers have Abstract Conceptualization (AC) as their predominant learning style. AC is learning by thinking. One uses logical analysis of ideas, systematic planning, and acts on intellectual understanding. So as the results indicate, it is seen that managers learn more by forming concepts, planning out things and using a lot of analysis before adopting it.

Active Experimentation learning style, as shown by 28 per cent of managers, is learning by doing, somewhere on the same lines as experiential learning. It is the ability to get things done, by taking risks and by influence people and events through action. These managers prefer taking the initiative, and doing work that is new and involves a lot of risk and excitement. They like to experiment on things before they adopt any strategy. This can be done by modeling a behaviour, analyzing it and then implementing it.

The 23 per cent of managers learn by Concrete Experience (CE). CE is involving oneself fully, openly, without bias in new experiences. It is learning from specific experiences, relating to people, sensitivity to feelings. It involves high levels of feeling and being engrossed in a task.

As for Reflective Observation (OR), 14 per cent managers have shown this as their mode of learning. OR is carefully observing before making judgment and viewing from different perspectives. These managers are more patient and while learning a new task they like to observe and draw their inferences from it. Also, they ask a lot of questions and clarify their doubts in the process.

Table 3

Learning Styles of Managers (N=120)

	Learning Styles			
Organisation No.	*Abstract Conceptualization*	*Active Experimentation*	*Concrete Experience*	*Reflective Observation*
1.	7	2	1	-
2.	4	-	2	4
3.	2	7	-	1
4.	-	-	7	3
5.	-	4	3	3
6.	7	2	1	-
7.	3	5	2	-
8.	1	4	3	2
9.	3	4	3	-
10.	3	2	3	2
11.	5		1	1
12.	7	1	1	1
Total	**42 (35%)**	**34(28%)**	**27(23%)**	**17(14%)**

The managerial psychology is most important in the study of organizational behaviour, as managers influence the organization most in terms of business and change management, organizational policies and strategies etc. Thus understanding of managerial behaviour is critical to the health of an organization for its existence, survival and excellence. Mumbai metro being a capital of trade and commerce, it is utmost important to know how its managers learn, lead and behave. Toward this objective, this study has provided certain guidelines.

Managers in Mumbai metro have been overused at the workplaces but less understood in terms of their psychological reactions and perceptions. Recently certain organizations have shown concern for managerial health by introducing yoga and stress management programmes. Lesser is known about the personality type, learning and leadership styles of managers in organizations.

The present study has been a good learning experience into the psychological aspects of life of managers. Managers were curious to know their personality type and an elabourative insight into it. Most managers shared that they practiced relaxation techniques like meditation, yoga, walks or some form of physical exercise to keep themselves fit and healthy. These gave them a good break from their hectic schedule and calmed their mind.

Leadership styles of manager is important to understand, the manner in which successful managers function and also, why they function, the way they do. They might be stern and authoritative, but there could be a reason behind it. The task of an Industrial Psychologist is to go in depth and understand why things happen rather than just obtaining an overview and jumping to conclusions. Most managers use authority because their job requires it. If they don't there will be an atmosphere of chaos and disorder around them.

The learning style provided knowledge of how successful managers grasp things for life. All learning styles are apt in their own way. Individual differences do exist, but it is interesting to know how each person has a unique style and goes about enhancing it to the fullest.

The study observations revealed that in each organization, there are a mix of people with transformational as well as transactional leadership styles, A as well as B personality type, and with different learning styles such as abstract conceptualization, active experimentation, concrete experience and reflective observation.

The predominant psychological constructs of managers in Mumbai are the transactional leadership style with A - personality type and learning styles as abstract conceptualization followed by active experimentation.

The majority of Mumbai managers are type A personality type (with 55 per cent A - and 20 per cent Type A personality types). People under this category are hardworking, ambitious and energetic. Managers under Type A personality often result in stress, heart ailments, and other coronary diseases. Type A's usually have high levels of competitiveness, ambition, workaholic attitude, irritable, restless with other's pace, reluctant to share power, over committed guilt over relaxing always works more than eight hours a day. These psychological constructs of managers can be attributed to its Mumbai's metropolitan nature of competitiveness, achievement motivation, and economic spirits.

A good match between individual personality and organization is essential. Mismatch between personality and organization structure may lead to stress, confusion and chaos loss of interest by members in the organization, low morale and job satisfaction.

Secondly, the most of Mumbai managers (65 per cent) fall under the style of transactional leadership.

Transactional leadership is built on reciprocity, the idea that the relationship between leader and their followers develops from the exchange of some reward, such as performance ratings, pay, recognition, and praise. It involves leaders clarifying goals and objectives, communicating to organize tasks and activities with the co-operation of their employees to ensure that wider organizational goals are met. Such a relationship depends on hierarchy and the ability to work through this mode of exchange. It requires leadership skills such as the ability to obtain results, to control through structures and processes, to solve problems, to plan and organize, and work within the structures and boundaries of the organization.

Transformational leadership, on the other hand, is concerned with engaging the hearts and minds of others. It works to help all parties achieve greater motivation, satisfaction, and a greater sense of achievement. It requires trust, concern and facilitation rather than direct control. The skills required are concerned with establishing a long-term vision, empowering people to control themselves, coaching, and developing others and challenging the culture to change. In transformational leadership, the power of the leader comes from creating understanding and trust. In contrast, in transactional leadership power is based much more on the notion of hierarchy and position.

Thus we can see that these two styles are starkly opposite in nature. A blend of these two styles might be the best option because it would be suited to the need of the situation and thus adaptable to the changing demands of a dynamic work force. Leadership is crucial to the achievement of high performance and essential in helping others aspire to and attain high levels of performance for themselves and the organization.

Thirdly, the predominant learning style of Mumbai managers is 'abstract conceptualization' which means they are people who adapt and integrate observations into complex but logically sound theories. They think problems through in a vertical step-by-step logical way. They assimilate disparate fact into coherent theories. They tend to be perfectionists who don't rest easy until things are tidy and fit into their rational scheme.

Learning is part of work and work involves learning; these are not separate functions but intertwined; the separation we have made of them is artificial and often does not serve us well. Learning is about obtaining correct information or answers from knowledgeable others; it is fundamentally about making meaning out of the experience others and we have in the world. Organizational learning results from planned efforts to learn. As a collective we are capable of learning our way to the answers we need to address our difficult problems.

The major highlights of the study can be summed up as under:

1. Personality type A - is more prevalent among managers.
2. Learning styles of abstract conceptualization followed by active experimentation are more common among managers.

3. Transactional style of leadership is more predominant among Mumbai managers.

As transactional style of leadership is more prevalent among Mumbai managers, it can be said that most of the managers see their job as managing, leading their employees, rewarding and intervening when the work standards are not met. They don't find themselves providing a vision or mental stimulation to employees for rising to further heights. The transactional style of leaders are more into managing and less into developing the potential of their employees and taking them to higher level of performance. The managers should make time for the development of the organization.

Transformational style of leadership is required for inculcating willingness to innovate, openness to change and creativity among the employees. As the progressive and globalising organizations are changing fast, they would require transformational leaders for introduction and management of change in the organizations. As transactional leaders are more comfortable with routine kind of activity maintenance, the metropolitan cities like Mumbai that is on the fast track of change, needs more transformational leaders.

The managers combining type A-personality type, 'active experimentation[1] learning style and transformational leadership style are the real change agents. These managers would guide the employees towards organizational goals. As personality A - type of the managers are more stress prone, they should be aware of their health sensitiveness and health maintenance. They need to take time out to relax as they don't distinguish between family and work life. They are like workaholics. Good health leads to better work and a prospering organization.

According to Sashikant Garware, Chairman, Garware Polyester, leaders are neither made in colleges nor born and today leadership necessarily will have to be multi-dimensional and multi-faceted like a diamond. Today's leaders have to determine their priorities along with three value dimensions– to perform, to reform and to conform, in the present fast changing environment on corporate value systems.

In view of the fast changing world around, the management education institutions and industry must prepare its potential managers into transformational leaders, good conceptualizers as well as active experimenters, and health conscious type A managers. This combination of managerial characteristics will make them real change ambassadors, implementers and help them adapt to the inevitably globalising corporate world. The learning and performing organizations may take a clue from this research for an inch of a step forward towards excellence, for a difference in excellence is measured in inches not miles.

References

Ahmad S; Varghese AR (1991). Learning Styles of Indian Managers: Some Explorations. *Journal of the Indian Academy of Applied Psychology*, 17(1-2), 55-9.

Bass, Bernard M (1997). Does the Transactional-Transformational Leadership Paradigm Transcend Organizational and National Boundaries? *The American Psychologist*, 52, (2), 130-139.

Bass, B.M., Avolio, B.J., Jung, D.I., Berson, Y. (2003). Predicting Unit Performance by Assessing Transformational and Transactional Leadership. *Journal of Applied Psychology*, 88, (2), 207-218.

Burns, J. M. (1978). *Leadership*. New York: Harper & Row.

Farley Frank (1990). The Big T in Personality, Farley Frank-University of Wisconsin-Madison, and Psychology Today, May 1990 article-Thrill Seeking often produces the Best Achievers but it can also Create the Worst Criminals.

Kaila, H.L. (2002). Stress is a Way of Life for Mumbai Workers, *Psychology International*, Vol. 13, No. 3, Fall 2002.

Kaila, H.L. (2003). How Do Metro Managers Cope With Their Stresses, And Health Problems? *The Journal of Health Management*, 5,1, 2003, 139-144.

Khurana Rakesh, The Curse of the Superstar CEO, Assistant Professor of OB in HBS, Boston. *Harvard Business Review*, September 2002.

Kolb, D. (1985). *Learning style inventory*. Boston, MA: McBer and Company.

Kolb, D; Rubin, I.M. and James, M. (1997). *Organizational psychology: An Experience to Organizational Behaviour*. Prentice Hall: New Jersey.

Manning, T.T. (2002). Gender, Managerial Level, Transformational Leadership And Work Satisfaction. *Women in Management Review*, 17, (5), 207-216.

Pestonjee D.M. (2001). *Stress and Coping: The Indian Experience 2nd edition*, Sage Publications.

Salgado (1997). Universal predictors of employee success-Five-Factor Personality Model, Five Factor Model of Personality and Job Performance in the European Community, *The Journal of Applied Psychology*, Vol. 82, No. 1, pp. 30-43.

Sarros, J.C. and Santora, J.C. (2001). The Transformational-Transactional Leadership Model in Practice. *Leadership and Organization Development Journal* 22, 383-394.

Susan Dawe (2002). Evaluating Training and Learning Practices in Large Firms, National Centre for Vocatonal Education Research Ltd., Paper presented at the 2002 Australsian Evaluation Society International Conference October/ November 2002-Wollongong Australia.

3

Stresses, Health Problems, and Coping Mechanisms of HR Managers

Managers at various levels direct the institutions, be it the industry, banks, hospitals, films, or the finance sector. Health of these managers is important for health of the organization and its business. Therefore, it is important to understand the managers' stresses, health problems, and how do they cope up with the work pressures in a more elabourate and specific manner.

A Human Resource (HR) Manager assists organizations to develop and implement policies relating to staff recruitment, industrial relations, training, and development of staff. They view people as an important source or asset to be used for the benefit of organization, employees, and the society. Thus, Managers' health is relevant for healthy development of the organizations, as they govern the institutions at various levels.

Hence, this section is especially earmarked to understand the stresses and health problems of HR managers, and importantly how do they cope with the human resource capital. In order to comprehend these, one hundred HR managers (70 males and 30 females, 86 married and 14 unmarried, age group 23-58) from 72 organizations (see appendix) at different positions were interviewed; the results are as follows:

- Stresses at work as HR manager
- Nature of health problems due to work pressures
- How do HR managers cope with their stresses?
- Summary

Stresses at Work as HR Manager

The managers expressed their stresses as follows:

- "It is extremely difficult to prove improvements gained through behavioural programmes. It causes stress to adhere to schedule and we should be very clear and good at communication."
- "Only constant factor in this profession is a 'change'. This constant change in demands builds up stress."
- "Making contacts and interacting with people successfully is a great challenge."
- "We often have the problem of providing skilled personnel as per the required qualifications for offshore projects. Due to this we face a big problem in visa processing."
- "Meeting deadlines and overcoming resistance when implementing HR policies are the chief stresses and challenges I face."
- "Implement things, to see whether things are running according to the objective of the project, how we can reduce cost and satisfy both internal and external customer to overcome resistance to change are my stresses."
- "Selection is hectic, as it's difficult to choose the best worker. Stress is often while arranging training programs for employees."
- "A lot of multitasking is required."
- "To manage whole organization with the help of different people in the organization. All people differ in their attitudes, thoughts, so everyone's participation is needed in each activity. Bring them all together is biggest challenge, stress at work due to changed work-culture, organization adopting different newer policies, and application of these policies create many stresses."
- "As a HR assistant we always deal with people. The main challenge is to understand them and assign different tasks to them according to their aptitudes, abilities, solving

different disputes. This task is very challenging and many stresses are involved. But as a human resource manager there are various responsibilities."

- "Selecting the right people is tough, as they are not available easily."
- "I don't face too many stresses; challenges are faced when the turnover is not good by the end of the year."
- "Sometimes meeting deadlines of projects becomes very tedious and affects my health."
- "There was too much of workload with a lot of pressures from superiors initially. But now I am used to it."
- "There is no hierarchical system, thus pressure does not occur."
- "Keeping human resources congruent with the risk management tools adopted is a continuous management challenge, e.g., understanding and the reasoning of the entire management team and changing risk management tools. An important part of the strategy for dealing with risk, e.g., creativity of people to deal with the unexpected, working with more people and more people."
- "If I like the work which I am doing then, no problem otherwise I have lots of tensions and stresses."

The Ten Major Stresses of HR Manager

1. Meeting deadlines
2. Making decisions
3. Selecting personnel
4. Retaining competent people
5. Peoples' problems
6. Multi-tasking
7. Long hours of work
8. Coordination of resources
9. Being cost- effective
10. Internal politics

The individual stresses of HR Managers are spelled out as below:

- Achieve targets, take comments from seniors
- Any new work becomes a challenge
- Attracting and retaining talent, being cost-effective, performance oriented transparent and fairness in approach
- Being a people person all the time
- Being parallel to the needs of one's changing organization
- Being responsible for making decisions for the better of the company
- Biggest challenge is to understand the needs of other people through right kind of policies, systems, practices in the organization.
- Catering to the needs of a company efficiently
- Coaching people to do things in a particular way on their own.
- Competition in the market, no security, long working hours.
- Conducting interviews
- Conflicts with staff members, supervisory problems, and union regularly
- Coordination of onsite and offsite resources.
- Dealing with different people
- Dependence on others to get your work done, expectations of people
- Employee management, their responses to change in work environment
- Ensure that all members of the organization work together with a shared purpose
- Excessive paperwork, administrative problems
- Facing new market challenges and adapting to a rapidly changing scenario
- Getting the right candidate in a short of time

- Handling empowerment and its proper implementation as employees' definition of empowerment does vary within an organization. Productivity is also another area, which poses a challenge.
- Handling people and their emotional needs is a big challenge
- Have to be flexible, good communication skills
- Identifying the right person, developing new selection techniques matching with requirements
- Innovations, creativity, overtimes, hectic schedules
- Interface with people at different levels, understanding their problems, union interference.
- Internal politics, dealing with people in a satisfactory manner.
- Job overload, traveling
- Know what is required, communicating with the people, downsizing (stress)
- Long working hours, out of station operations forces you to stay away from family
- Lot of patience on your part is required
- Lot of stress due to work and no conducive work environment
- Maintaining performance development, lack of planning
- Man-management, high expectations, policies to be designed, dealing with a large number of people, and even unpleasant situations.
- Managing people and dealing with their problems
- Meet deadlines, planning effective programs and making decisions
- Motivation and morale building and developing new competencies.
- Overtime, working at odd hours
- Performance management
- Prioritizing and meet deadlines, analyze situation before hand
- Retain the talented workforce. Motivate the workers, devise new methods, satisfying workers' demands

- Shift work related problems
- Sourcing and retaining competent managers, improving work cultures, making unions and workers accountable, resolving surplus manpower problem
- Staff management, routine work
- Strain of excessive paperwork
- Support business, slight politics, how to convince people about the value of HRD
- Time management problem and stress due to work pressure
- Training workforce for better productivity, satisfying growing demands of workers and motivating them
- Value creation, increasing competency levels, changing mindsets

The above responses indicate that there are stresses of different nature being experienced by HR staff in their respective organizations. Though there is a commonality in stress experience, there is uniqueness too depending upon the needs of the situation. These stress perceptions of the managers also indicate that they need to equip themselves as per demands made by the employees and the management.

Nature of Health Problems Due to Work Pressures (Physical and Psychological)

HR managers expressed their health problems as below:

- "One has to be happy with work pressure hence there is no place for health problem due to work pressure."
- "Sometimes due to high work pressure, I have to face headaches, acidity etc."
- "Mental pressure is always there when a hard decision is taken."
- "I have migraines and sometimes sinus but I am not sure whether it is due to work pressure."
- "There are no physical problems but a lot of mental stress as one needs to take a lot of decision, I know that I am

doing something wrong to somebody and this causes lot of stress. Generally work is in office, so many HR people become fat by sitting all the time."

- "Stress related health problems. But these can not be ruled out in other functions, however, since HR is human sensitive has broader responsibility, feeling of dejection sometimes leads to problems."
- "Due to stress lower, back pain, burning eyes, inadequate sleep, these permanent members are always there."
- "I get back pains as most of the time I have to sit in front of the computer which also leads to severe headaches."
- "I experience lack of sleep and neck and back aches."
- "I experience high blood pressure sometimes."

Ten Major health problems of HR Managers:

- Aches in the neck
- Acidity, indigestion, gastric problems
- Back pain
- Blood pressure problems
- Fatigue
- Headaches
- Lack of sleep
- Short tempers
- Spondilitis
- 20 per cent do not experience any health problems

Individual Health Problems as reported by individual HR managers:

- Anxiety and lack of sleep
- Backaches, headaches, insomnia
- Blood pressure
- Constant headaches
- Eye pressure due to computer
- Fatigue

- Frequent headaches and cold
- High blood pressure
- High stress levels
- Indigestion, gastric problems
- Long working hours, lack of sleep, leading to short temper
- Lower-back pains
- Migraine and sometimes un-stable behaviour
- Mounting pressures, diabetes, eyesight, and blood pressure problems.
- Neck tension
- Nothing, because I enjoy the work
- Occasional tension, headache and feeling of exhaustion
- Restlessness
- Short tempers, mood swings.
- Sleeping problem, pain in the back and neck
- Spondilitis and back pain.
- Stomach upset
- Stress–physical and mental

The above data reveal that the health problems of the HR managers are largely psychosomatic in nature. They are alarming in the sense that if the managers themselves or the respective organizations do not take corrective measures; it might cost huge in terms of health impairment of the managers resulting in lowered organizational performance. The health of managers is equal to health of the organization as they influence the significant decisions concerning the organizational growth and development.

How do HR Managers Cope with their Stresses?

The HR managers expressed their Coping Styles as below:

- "I really enjoy facing the day to day changes and consider this as challenge."

- "I regularly go for a walk in the morning before my day. It relaxes my mind, it also provides freshness to my mind sometimes I listen music."
- "I often become stressed because of work pressure; I prefer listening music, reading books, sometimes I do yoga."
- "We have to keep very high level of moral and motivation. Mental flexibility and positive attitude help to achieve desired objectives."
- "It is being taking care through experience and correct decision at appropriate time."
- "I keep faith that I can complete my work on time and do all the best, which I can."
- "We have to consider what impact our decision will take on the organization, and should not think only in terms of one person. It needs lot of convincing and pushing, very good communication skills and ability to visualize."
- "Trying to focus on my goals and think positive as that helps one to overcome all obstacles that are work related."
- "I am a very short-tempered person, meditation is a good relief. I take the challenges as they come."
- "I try to divide my workload in the office hours. I try and give priorities to work and avoid extra work."
- "I really enjoy facing the day to day changes and consider this as challenge."
- "I communicate and talk with colleagues."
- "I do yoga in the morning, I feel better almost 3-4 days, I do it along with it great relief is provided by reading books also news paper cuttings."
- "I restrict my challenges and stress only to office and do not carry them home. I spend time with family and relax myself."
- "I take break from work and engage myself in some other work or surf not. After office hours I hang out with my friends and overcome tensions."

Ten Major Coping Styles of HR managers:

- Exercise
- Meditation
- Prioritizing work
- Reading
- Relaxation
- Talking with colleagues
- Team work
- Time management
- Training courses
- Yoga

Individual Coping Styles of HR managers

- Attending personnel development courses
- Avoiding procrastination
- Believe that the thing that is being done is right, no negative feeling, if there is negative feeling then we can't work. Try to do as good as possible, keep your calm and convincing people about issues.
- Channeling resources
- Consulting seniors, colleagues and subordinates
- Continuous learning, reading etc, by yoga and meditation
- Co-operative team work
- Depends on what type of challenge I face
- Discussing problems with co-workers
- Doing best by being objective
- Doing lot of research work
- Effective training courses offered by the company
- Exercise, yoga, meditation
- Family support
- Find innovative ideas to make the work better
- Find week challenging.

- Finishing work on time, allocating a little for relaxing between work
- Good communication skills
- Have to meet many candidates, which is time consuming. I have a chart on how I should manage time effectively
- Just try and finish work
- Keep abreast of all news
- Keep at it; not think much about it
- Keep in constant touch with what's working and what's not, spending time with employees
- Long walks
- Making replacement then and there
- Meditating, exercising and watching movies
- Optimization approach to solve problem, transparency in work profile, open communication
- Planning the work properly, team work, otherwise I spend my time in sudarshan kriya activities.
- Prioritizing work, planning strategically, being focused, targeting the right mass
- Projecting a positive attitude and sending mailers to all on such topics like positive thinking how to cope with stress and such related topics.
- Reading work related matters, exercising – aerobics, swimming etc.
- Relaxation techniques, yoga
- Sleep as much as time permits
- Social interactions
- Swimming
- Take a break
- Taking it as life goes on
- Taking proper decisions
- Talking it out
- Team work

- Time management and systematic organized programs
- Try to put things in a positive and non-defensive way.
- Updating knowledge by continuously reading and trying to apply those strategies in practice
- Weekend detonation.

As it can be seen above, these coping strategies and skills being used by the managers in order to fight their stresses or to re-energize them are varied in nature. Some of these coping mechanisms are quick stress relievers or solutions, whereas other techniques are enabling and empowering in nature.

Summary

The stresses that HR managers (at the middle, senior and top level) experience are: meeting deadlines, making decisions, selecting personnel, retaining competent people, managing peoples' problems, multi-tasking, long hours of work, coordination of resources, being cost-effective, and internal politics.

Their physical and psychological health problems are fatigue, headaches, acidity, lack of sleep, blood pressure problems, spondilitis, back pain, aches in the neck, and short tempers. The 20 per cent of HR managers do not experience any health problems.

The strategies of coping stress that the HR managers use are: relaxation, reading, meditation, talking with colleagues, yoga, attending training courses, time management, team work, exercise, and prioritizing work.

And finally, the most important functions of HR managers are to deal successfully with people, and to ensure the availability and maximize the use of a competent workforce to an organization for better business results. In order for them to deliver to these expectations, the organizations need to take steps to ensure both the physical and mental health of HR managers so that they can contribute towards the development of the healthy organizations and a better business environment.

4
The Current HR Scenario

A survey of ninety Irish high technology companies revealed that 95 per cent of companies had an established HRD function; 81 per cent had a written HRD policy statement. In addition to which it was found that the individuals identified as being responsible for implementing the HRD plan varied widely: 41 per cent saw it as the sole responsibility of the HRD manager, 35 per cent indicated that it was the responsibility of the HRD specialist and the line manager, 8 per cent the line manager only and 16 per cent the human resource manager. Some organizations have impressive training plans, which result in little development of the staff while others may have little in the way of elabourate HRD plans and experience development at all levels. Essentially what creates the difference between them is the identification of the skill performance gap by able HR professionals who then capitalize on internal forces for change and minimize the restraining forces from both within and outside the organization creating successful, innovative organizations (Thomson, R. and Mabey, C. 1994).

Braham, J. (1994) is of the view that for many employees the suspicion remains that HR is another device, the latest fad to provide a moral cloak of respectability concealing the true purpose of business, i.e., to reduce costs and make a fast buck. However, there should be little doubt that a HR manager or professional within an organization plays a crucial role. While team building camps and the like are enjoyable learning experiences they do not necessarily translate to commitment. The HR function is therefore to persuade managers to drop the traditional approaches to people and work towards a position of mutuality and trust. The HR manager must guard against a dependence on fads, the main question being whether the suggested new technique is simply a repackaging of an old one or whether it provides a change of real substance. Many organizations look at the cost of recruitment, training etc. and come to the decision that they can save by getting someone outside the organization to contract for the task. However the HR manager will be working on people management strategies that are central to the organization and cannot be out-sourced. Finally HR managers should beware of fashionable HR speak.

The Vice President HR, Mr. Srihar found that the line dividing ethical and unethical behaviour was fast becoming fuzzy at Seeps India. The only thing that seemed to matter was success even if that meant bypassing decency. An employee Ms. Beena was found to be very effective at media networking but her interaction with the senior and junior staff was less than satisfactory. Srihar discovered that during a brain storming session she had shot down the ideas of the senior staff. Moreover in order to rid them of competition, marketing managers at Seeps let slip to staff citing the media that a competitor was evading excise duties. The competitor lost its footing in the market as a result. As the head of HR, Srihar sought to take on the management over the growing epidemic of unethical practices. The case analysis provided by experts pointed out that at Seeps there was an overlooking of personal values and reiterated that organizations have to be run in ways which people value - what they consider to be 'good' or 'worthy'. Furthermore they pointed out that corporate success stories have been those of companies which have been value driven (Gangee, Z; and Sengupta, U. 1999).

Taking lead from the above HR issues, this section has been organized to address the four fundamental issues or questions that challenge the HR executive in the organizations today. This includes:

- What is the nature of work of a HR executive?

- What are the work challenges as a HR executive?
- How does a HR executive cope with these challenges?
- How does a HR executive perceive of the HRD scenario as a whole?

In order to examine, address, and contextualize these issues, it is important to first understand the views of a personnel manager and the HR executives of certain companies as below:

Views of a Personnel Manager of a Chemicals Company

The aim of HR development is to build organization, improve its performance, show its concern for human dignity, and a quest for excellence. HR development means the development of:

- Coherent thinking
- Problem-solving ability
- Consensus-obtaining ability
- Depth of insight
- Technical and conceptual skills
- Reading habits
- Capacity to look inward
- Tenacity to live of dissent
- Integrity

HR development is essentially a process of:

- Transforming the organizational climate in which knowledge will be appreciated
- Providing experiential learning for the improvement of performance by self study; self development through gradual abdication of ego-centrism
- Acquiring skills by tapping talents trapped within oneself by antiquated attitudes; and
- Self-realization by trying to understand who am I from the point of view of motivation and satisfaction.

Nature of Work of a HR Executive

The 100 HR managers (from 72 diverse companies) during the interviews expressed their nature of work as follows:

- "Being head of HR, my job consists of various works like interviews, recruitment regarding different cells in the organizations. Different training programs are arranged."
- "Working in the human resource department is very interesting work. As it involves recruitment, performance appraisal, interviews, training programs. We often take meetings for interaction between employees and their managers."
- "Entire training is taken care of (identification to actual training), statutory provisions, welfare of employees, administration, appraisal, promotions, increments."
- "Our work involves job analysis and job descriptions, hiring, orientation and training, employer/employee interaction, performance appraisal, compensation, discipline, etc."

Ten Major HR Activities

- Budgeting
- Job analysis and Recruitment
- Induction
- Training and development
- Career planning
- Framing of policies
- Compensation and related issues
- Performance Appraisals
- Exits
- HR audit

The Individual HR Managers spelled out their nature of job as below:

- Advising management on corrective and disciplinary actions, representing an organization in appeals or grievances, conducting labour negotiations, mediation or arbitration, organizational analysis or development, interpretation and application of laws, rules, policies and procedures, and other personnel services.

- Annual medical leave for employees.
- Assist in conducting development workshops for sales, interviewing performance appraisals.
- Classification, compensation, selection, affirmative action, diversity, staff and leadership development and training, career counseling, employee recognition and motivation, abort negotiations and salary arbitration, as well as helping to develop ongoing staff-management communication strategies and monitor both the need for, and effectiveness of, professional development and training programs.
- Conducting training programs for the employees.
- Consulting, Communication and Interpersonal Interaction, Analysis and Problem Solving, Advice and counsel, Employee advocacy, hiring, training, employee relations, systems analysis and management.
- Coordination and maintaining good inter-departmental negatiations, dealing with employee problems, training.
- Corporate HR training.
- Designing and formulation of strategies and their implementation. Constant touch/dialogue with people.
- Developing and advising Corporate on Behavioural Sciences and HR policy.
- Employee redressal, exit interviews, job evaluation description related administration.
- Employee relationship management.
- Finance and accounts functions besides HRD and administration functions like conducting interview, pay roll activities, pay structure and gradation, increment, promotions, conducting in-house training.
- Formulation and implementation of HR policies.
- Growth and development and people processes.

- Handling all departments.
- Handling Personnel problems.
- Handling personnel, industrial relations of all corporate houses of group of companies.
- HR activities; recruiting, appraisals, communication etc.
- HR audit, administrative process, improvement management.
- Interaction with union, welfare and statutory activities, training activities, ISO activities.
- Internal events: festivals, sports competition, annual day, Christmas mass, parties Inter-games, medical welfare activities coordinator welfare trust.
- Interpreting rules and policies to direct payroll actions, explaining human resource policies, procedures, and programs to employees, managers, the public, providing technical assistance to support the professional responsibilities completing requests for personnel actions, benefits, providing training or orientation in area of responsibility; maintaining confidential records and generating reports.
- ISO Adherence .
- Joining formalities, insurance, payroll, disciplinary action, formulation of local standard operating reports (monthly).
- Manpower planning, personnel activities.
- Marketing the services of the firm.
- Motivating the work force and maintaining balance between the workers demands and company's profit.
- OB, IR, administration of personnel.
- Organizational development, organizational survey, employee policies, training.
- Performance management, manpower planning.
- Personnel administration, overseeing training programmes and the like.
- Personnel selection and staffing.

- Planning training programmes, carrying out activities like performance appraisal.
- Planning, coordination, organizing things for administration, interviews, training people, coaching, and feedback.
- Preparing need analysis of training and planning HR strategies.
- Provide leadership in mentoring, establishing the vision, and strategy for the hiring organization for planning, coordinating, directing, and job placement activities.
- Recruiting personnel for company through interviews and professional aptitude test.
- Roster scheduling.
- Selection–interviewing candidates.
- Supervising internal events–festivals, competitions, annual day, parties, employee welfare / medical activities, disciplinary action, salaries - rewards, punishments, awards.
- To get the work done in time and to give our best to the client.
- To keep the moral of our employees high.

The above description of individual HR Managers about their nature of job in diverse organizations indicates that though there are certain common roles and responsibilities of the HR personnel, different organizations employ HR Managers for different organizational requirements.

Challenges of HR Managers

The challenges that the HR managers face at the work places are as below:

- Facing new market challenges and adapting to a rapidly changing scenario. Motivation and morale building and developing new competencies. Being parallel with the needs of changing organization.
- Handling people and their emotional needs is a big challenge. To ensure that all members of the organization work together with a shared purpose is another very big challenge.

- Keeping human resources congruent with the risk management tools adopted is a continuous management challenge, e.g., the entire management team's understanding the reasoning for changing risk management tools, maintaining performance development. Strategic partnership impacts work positions; hiring; reward, recognition, and strategic pay; performance development and appraisal systems; career and succession planning; and employee development. One needs to become more adaptable, resilient, and quick to change direction.
- Planning keeping in mind both employee and organizational constraints as far as possible in order to create excellence in performance. Planning and seeking to implement innovative HR policies, dialogue with employees etc. Cope up by communicating and from earlier learning.

How do HR Executive Cope with these Challenges?

HR executives cope with these challenges through:

- Communication
- Conflict management
- Evaluation
- Interviewing
- Leadership
- Motivation
- Teaching and training
- Working with more and more people affects strategic decisions. An important part of the strategy is dealing with risk through creativity of people to deal with the unexpected.
- By fostering effective methods of goal setting, communication, and empowerment through responsibility build employee ownership of the enterprise. Planning, hiring, training, communication, and discipline practices mold the work force.
- By strategic policy planning and ensuring that all line managers adopt its principles as a part of their everyday work.

How do HR Executives Perceive the HRD Scenario

HR managers expressed their perceptions as follows:

- "I am working in this field since many years. It is very challenging and interesting task. Everyday is a new day for us. Everyday we learn something new and we always try to practically apply it because in today's competitive world practical application matters. Due to this work I always can enrich myself as a competitive and definitely as a effective leader who can lead and help others and organizations development."
- "HR department is very important but it still has a long way to go in India."
- "Very upbeat, our organization has been certified PCMM level 5 and we as HRD staff always strive to better ourselves everyday and keep ourselves open to new ideas."
- "The definition of work is constantly changing, as is the relationship between employer and employee. Organizations, which value and plan HR functions well will benefit in the long run while those, which do not will still function reasonably well though perhaps not at optimum efficiency."
- "Creating a committed workforce is the main function of the HR professional in any organization today. HRD however has its skeptics. Through proper implementation of policies and well-trained professionals to aid the process an acceptance of HR will gradually occur among employees."
- "It's a very important department because the company's reputation depends on the quality of people working in it, and our job starts right from recruiting to selection to training to the end that is termination, etc."

Ten Major Perceptions of HR Managers

- HR is as important as any other department
- HR has to be more business oriented
- It's lifeline of an organization

- It's integral to the success of a firm
- Its competitive and challenging
- It has to keep in tandem with growing industry
- Is very satisfying and high dignity attained to it
- It is very important to maintain good internal atmosphere.
- A necessity for every organization
- Vital part—backbone of an organization.

Individual perception of HR Managers are spelled out below:

- A very important part of any business, HRD undertakes all the crucial activities which enables an organization to run smooth.
- An integral part and a must for every organization.
- As important and vital as any department.
- As people and their skills become an ever more valuable part of every business, the need for human resource professionals can only grow.
- Challenging, hectic, competitive and critical dept.
- Excellent creative novel, opportunity to meet a lot of people.
- Fast growing and extremely promising.
- Future CEO's would emerge from this dept.
- H.R.D. is a backbone of the organization is being well recognized now.
- H.R.D. is a very interesting field with lots to do in it.
- H.R.D. is very important in an organization because organization depends upon human face.
- HR – totality of ability, talent, knowledge of the entire organization.
- HR function is as important as any other functions of the organization.
- HR has to be more business oriented.

- HR is integral part of an organization, it has to understand business needs.
- HR is very crucial aim of any organization, it is crucial. right from recruitment to an employees exit.
- HR is well accepted as we have good systems here in place.
- HR plays a major role in any organization to the extent in identifying the strength and weakness of market and helping in providing solutions.
- HR plays a significant role in the organization. We need to keep pace with the time and work as a team member.
- HRD is a business partner - 100 per cent utility of all aspects will help in saving the resources, thus profit.
- HRD is still evolving and empowering employees; team working and commitment is the need of the hour.
- HRD scenario is too hyped. As HR managers we need to have experience of sales and marketing to be able to recruit.
- HRD views employees as internal guests, and HR manager is like an internal police dealing with negations in the organization and coordination of staff and management.
- Integral part of organization.
- Is very satisfying and high dignity attained to it.
- It is a very important point without which an organization cannot be said to be complete.
- It is now a force to be work with still growing.
- It is of excessive importance for keeping the employees welfare, maintaining discipline and a congenial atmosphere.
- It is the back bone of the Call Center Industry.
- It is very important for every organization for giving more and deserved attention to employees.
- It needs lot more business perspectives. One should know is business.

- It's integral to the success of a firm.
- It's very responsible job. Since in my company we have monthly status update report for every employee, it provides our needs for making further personal development.
- It's challenging right from paper work to interaction with operations.
- Its gaining a lot importance lately and its importance is growing slowly, an upcoming field. Its very challenging, flourishing, will have even scope in future in India.
- Most important function in any organization without which one cannot survive.
- Powerful department can do wonders for company.
- There are lots of new processes and systems to be implemented in HRD. Keep learning new things and lots of opportunity to grow.
- There exists much scope for improvement through the use of innovative policies.

The HR scenario as expressed by the HR managers reveals the multiple facets of human resource departments in the Indian organizations. This is a very important field, which recognizes the organization goals and tries to meet them. It's very important function, important to get best performance, lifeline of an organization. There are mixed expressions, which indicate that the HR field is being experienced differently by the respective managers. It's certainly a challenge to the human resource professional in a globalising business scenario. Its evolving and has to keep in tandem with growing industry. Unleashing potential and creativity is the main HR function. Valuing human resources and aligning as closely as possible employee and organizational goals will create an atmosphere conducive to growth and development.

Some examples of the nature of work, challenges, coping style, and perception of HR managers

Example 1

Nature of work	Learning and Development
Challenges at work as HR Manager	Deadline, Deliverables and Commitments
How do you cope up with these challenges?	By having a positive mental attitude
Perception of HRD in organizations	Positive

Example 2

Nature of work (processes involved)	Chiefly personnel administration, overseeing training programmes and the like.
What are the challenges you face at work as HR manager?	Meeting deadlines and overcoming resistance when implementing HR policies are the chief stresses and challenges I face.
How do you cope wi these challenges?	Through time management, proper planning and control of HR functions.
What is your perception of HRD in organizations?	The definition of work is constantly changing, as is the relationship between employer and employee. Organizations, which value and plan HR functions well will benefit in the long run · while those, which do not will still function reasonably well though perhaps not at optimum efficiency.

Example 3

Nature of work (processes involved)	Human Resource Management-overseeing training, selection etc.
What are the challenges you face at work as HR manager?	Mainly handling empowerment and its proper implementation as employees' definition of empowerment does vary within an organization. Productivity is also another area which poses a challenge

How do you cope with these challenges?	Planning is the key to coping with challenges that arise as well as strategic handling of human resources.
What is your perception of HRD in organizations?	There exists much scope for improvement through the use of innovative policies.

Example 4

Nature of work (processes involved)	Developing and advising Corporate on Behavioural Sciences and HR policy.
What are the challenges and stresses you face at work as a HR manager?	Value creation, increasing competency levels, changing mindsets.
How do you cope with these challenges?	Keeping an open mind and having constant dialogue and interaction with employees across the board.
What is your perception of HRD in organizations?	Unleashing potential and creativity is the main HR function. Valuing human resources and aligning as closely as possible employee and organizational goals will create an atmosphere conducive to growth and development.

Summary

Creating a committed workforce is the main function of the HR professional in any organization today. The HR professional contributes to the organization by constantly assessing the effectiveness of the human resources. He / she also sponsors change in other departments and in work practices. To promote the overall success of the organization, he / she champions the identification and implementation of the organizational mission, vision, values, goals, and action plans.

Human Resource Management has come a long way and the companies are stressing the importance of people. Peoples' skills have become an ever more valuable part of every business. The human resource professionals have been increasingly recognized in organizations. HR has become a very crucial department because the company's reputation depends on the quality of people working in it, and HR job starts right from recruiting to selection to training to the end that is termination. Through proper implementation of policies and well-trained professionals to aid the process, an acceptance of HR professionals has risen among the organizations and employees.

The human resource activities have widened its scope to include crucial HR issues related to recruitment, performance appraisal, communication, decision making, group processes, job satisfaction, leadership, organizational development interventions, training effectiveness, organizational culture, women managers, mentoring and coaching, HRM in NGOs, and international human resource management.

Today management of human resource is vital to every company and industry. It is the responsibility of HR professionals to make sure that the employees, managers, and the company are performing efficiently and effectively. As HRD is evolving and empowering employees, team working and commitment are the need of the hour.

5

The New Human Resource Professional

The previous section has dealt with the four fundamental issues that challenge the HR executive in the organizations such as nature of work of a HR executive, the work challenges as a HR executive, the way HR executive cope with these challenges, and HR executive perception's of the HRD scenario.

This section is based on the conclusions that have emerged from the interview responses of 100 HR managers from 72 companies (see Appendix–Organizations). It highlights different features of the new HR professional such as the emerging functions of HR managers, their major stresses and health problems, coping skills, the new trends, and the case analysis of HR managers etc.

Features of the New HR Professional

1. The Emerging Functions of HR Managers
2. Their Stresses
3. Health Problems HR Managers Face
4. Coping Skills
5. The Human Factor
6. A Balancing Act
7. The Insights of HR Managers
8. The New HR Department
9. HR is the Heart of the Organization
10. HRD is an Emerging Field
11. Case Analysis of HR Managers

12. The HR Women Manager
13. The First-Line Manager
14. Human Resources Redefined
15. Summary

The Emerging Functions of HR Managers

HR manager's functions involves activities like recruitment and selection, orientation and placement, training and development, performance appraisal and job evaluation, employee remuneration, motivation and communications, welfare, safety and health and the like, needed for a successful being of any organization. HR managers are concerned with people's dimension in organizations. They view people as an important source or asset to be used for the benefit of organization, employees, and the society. They aim at policies that promote mutuality – mutual goals, mutual respect, mutual rewards, and mutual responsibilities. The primary objective of HR is to ensure the availability of a competent and willing workforce to an organization. The most important quality of a HR manager is to deal successfully with people.

The nature of work process involved are found to be almost similar for all which include mainly recruitment, training, performance appraisal etc. the challenges and stresses vary a little which include job overload, traveling, performance, psychological burnout, decision making, dealing with people, recruitment of people etc but the most frequent report is of meeting deadlines. The coping strategies mainly include relaxation and managing time. They all perceive HRD as a crucial, vital, integral part of an organization.

Their overall work processes involved recruitment, joining formalities, payroll, disciplinary action, insurance, formulation of local operating reports, training – identification to the actual training, statutory provision, welfare of employees, administration, appraisals, promotions, increments, industrial relations, motivating workforce etc.

The Stresses

Their stresses at work as HR managers are noted to be the following: time management problem, stress due to work pressures, retaining the talented workforce, devise new methods, satisfying workers' demands. Improving work cultures, making unions and workers accountable, resolving surplus manpower problems etc.

Since their nature of work was different, the stresses that they faced were also different. But a common stress that was faced by many HR managers was meeting deadlines.

As the stresses of HR people differ from company to company, some of these specific stresses are: taking comments from seniors, achieving targets, internal politics, attracting and re-training talent, transparency, convincing people of the usefulness and value of HR etc.

Health Problems HR Managers Face

Most of the HR managers feel that they do not have any physical problems due to work pressure. Some of them face mental problems such as tensions; headache in the form of migraines, sometimes taking a hard decision also causes stress. Some other problems faced by HR managers include aches in lower back, neck or upper back, poor appetite, trouble getting to sleep, feeling nervous, fidgety or tense and becoming tired in a short period of time.

There were different health problems found, due to work, but they differed due to age of HR managers. One woman manager of 27 years happily expressed that she had no particular health problems. Besides her, everyone complained of following problems: Headaches, diabetes, eyesight problems, blood pressures, acidity, indigestion, gastric problems, spondilitis and back pains etc.

In general it can be said that, though job of HR managers is stressful, it does not lead to serious or even certain commonly occurring health problems. The reason for this could be many. One of the reasons could be that, HR managers' function is a staff function and not a line function. So, it is not directly related to the outcome of business. This may remove the immense work stress generally found in managers' performing line functions. Moreover, while interacting with these HR managers it was found that all of them enjoyed their jobs as it had a vast scope and large variety. All of them seemed to be satisfied and looking forward for challenges in their jobs. Therefore this positive attitude may be an important reason for very few health problems in HR managers.

Managers complain of trouble with sweaty hands, which feel clammy and damp. They also reported of being nervous, fidgety sometimes. The problem of aches in lower back was found often in the managers. They 'sometimes' have trouble with poor appetite. Some managers have getting to sleep and staying asleep. Managers in the higher age bracket (between age of 44 to 49 years) reported to have borderline high blood pressure problem.

The kind of health problems people had due to work were acidity, headaches and tiredness.

Major health hazards amongst HRD personnel are related to long working hours. Insomnia or trouble sleeping seems very common. Even short temper, temper outburst, mood swings are common place. Lack of appetite is also linked to long working hours.

The managers reported hypertension and blood pressure. A manager responded saying that it is caused due to pressure of meeting deadlines.

Coping Skills

Good communication skill was one of the ways of coping with the challenge. Other coping strategies included keeping a positive attitude and belief in oneself, ability to visualize the impact of the decisions made. Some of the qualities which HR managers should have were said by the interviewers to be good communication skills, practical knowledge, business sense, positive attitude and so on. The HR managers developed stress management skills to keep themselves healthy and fit.

Different people having different coping strategies, like the following: communication with colleagues, exercises, yoga, chanting, social interaction, one mentioned that he copes up with his stress by planning the work properly, team work, and besides this he spends time in SSY center and Sudarshan kriya activities. Other one mentioned that he restricts his stress only to office and does not carry home. He prefers relaxing with family. Other young manager says that he hangs out with his friends and overcome work tension.

The ways people cope is mainly team work keep doing your best, being positive and objective. The perception of HR of these people is pretty similar. Most felt that the role of HR was evolving it is now a necessary part of any organization. One went, as far to say that now HR people are also becoming CEOs and heads of companies.

The Human Factor

Though the managers dealt with a different aspect of HR such as corporate HR, administrative process, recruitment, performance management, manpower planning, corporate training and improvement management, the commonly faced challenge is dealing with people. HR deals with the human factor in the organization and whichever area of the department the person may be working in, it certainly involves a lot of interaction with people and therefore getting the work done through people was perceived as a challenge.

A Balancing Act

HR is an important function. It is the bridge between management and staff. HR tries to get a fit between job and the person. It also involves working with welfare units and builds the culture of the organization. These are a lot of new processes and systems to be implemented, lots of new things to learn and opportunities to grow. It needs business perspectives, HR managers should be aware of business policies and the way other areas of organization function. Expectations of HRD are quite high and it is the HRD, which has to keep a balance between people's demand and organizational policies.

The Insights of HR Managers

In the knowledge driven organization, HR plays a significant role as you are dealing with man and not machines; the sensitivities are at peaks in such organization. Human emotions, sensitivity, transparency, fairness are the key attributes where HR is looked at. HR has walked a long way from its role of Personnel Administration to Human Development. HR now plays a role of strategic partner in business discussions / framing. HR professionals have moved up to be the CEOs / Director's of the organization. In today's environment wherein more and more outsourcing of routine activities is being stressed upon, Personnel Administration in most of the organization is being out-sourced (viz., payroll, benefits/perk management, statutory requirement, etc.) HR now concentrates more and more on being strategic contributor in terms of business, its people requirement, right person at right time and at right place addressing developmental needs and softer issues etc. The HR managers expressed their insights as follows:

"HR is an important function. It is the bridge between management and staff, and it gives chance to the employees to empress their feeling. It works with welfare units culture of the organization is build by HR tries to get the fit between job and person making people by with their job."

"The HR department is responsible for the development of the human resources and taking care of the growth of these resources for the parallel development of the organization with the personal development."

"Expectations of HRD are quite high. HRD has to keep a balance between people's demand and organizational policies."

"Its vital in any organization, HRD is a connecting link between workforce and top management."

"HR is very important function in the organization. Being HR manager you have practice right kind of policies. People in the organization you have to father them you have to spot the right kind of people for Good performance in the organization. It gives that competitive edge in the organization. Satisfied employees can take care of your organization now organizations have began to feel or realize the importance performance appraisal interviews all are challenging tasks. It is a dynamic function."

"Human resource manager name itself tells the importance managing human resource effectively in the organization is a big challenge or at work place. To understand other people's overcoming problems, satisfy their demands by taking care of organization to be good human resource manager you should be a good psychologist also who can know others by thinking from their point of view."

The New HR Department

The HRD scenario is perceived to be challenging by the managers, because it extends right from paper works to interaction with operations. It's competitive in nature. It is a business partner – 100 per cent utility of all aspects will help in saving the resources, thus 'profit'. HRD is a connecting link between workforce and top management.

HR is competitive and demanding area; wherein there are lot of stresses, tensions, and challenges. HR managers generally, are the busiest workers in an organization; they undertake activities right from paper work to actual operations and conduction of seminars for the welfare of employees. They act as a mediator, between employees and management. They should be possessing positive attitude to handle the various ups and downs that they come across. Communication skills play a vital role in HR manager's life, because they help them get connected to people of different temperaments.

They have immense number of challenges to face, for example, structuring interviews, selecting suitable candidates, recruiting, training etc. They need to meet the demands of employees as well as make them happy. They have to be in the restrictions of company policies, laws, and jurisdiction and still keep employees satisfied and motivated to work. Due to continuos hours spent on desk, they develop lower back pains, tensions due to challenges etc. HR managers have hectic schedule full with work, work and just work for the human resource of their organization.

HR profession is highly looked at and individuals who are into it find it very satisfying and challenging. It is a very upcoming field; scope is wide with appropriate qualifications and experience. Its very interesting as it deals with human resources of organizations that are the wheels of any organization. The HRM challenges in the 2000's are manifold. With the complexity in the productive structure, the need for improving the effectiveness of human resources has become imperative. The changes in social, economic and technological conditions are affecting business and pose a major challenge to HR personnel. It is the task of the HR managers and other professionals to cope with these challenges of the strategic environment and create a niche for their organization.

The role of HR professionals in a new paradigm of business is to be redefined as the next millennium has set a very challenging task for HR managers. HR profession has changed due to changes taking place in business, caused by global competition, downsizing and technological advances. HR professionals are in a great flux due to workplace and socio-cultural changes taking place across the globe. The issues and priorities have to be explored and reviewed by HR managers, if they want to become a strategic partner in organizational growth and development. HR professionals are experiencing conflict due to forces currently, working within and outside the world of organization. The corporate world wants HR managers to play the role of a catalyst, and at the same time they also want them to cope up with the problems and issues related to workforce. There is also a realization that investment in people is an essential requirement for progress and development of organizations. Therefore HR managers have to rethink about their role. They have to plan, prioritize, and set goals for themselves.

HR managers have to understand the challenges and realities of the business, so that they can facilitate a smooth transition of organization and workforce in the next millennium. HR professionals have to do a strategic analysis of the changes taking place in the business environment. The major concern of HR professionals/managers will be to figure out how to build organizational capacity to maximize the potential of the business in the market place. HR had a pivotal role in the past, and will play a more critical role, as we move forward into the next century.

Organizations have changed due to restructuring and downsizing efforts. This has created new challenges for organizations. The major issues related to work environment such as flexibility, managing a diverse workforce, sexual harassment, AIDS, international workforce have created new challenges for HR professionals.

HR is the Heart of the Organization

As a result of introduction of new industrial relations and human resource management policies, human resource development policies presently are being integrated into the overall policies of the organization.

It is said that 'HRD is the heart of the industry.' Consequently the steps taken for the development of human resources become very important.

HR professionals are playing an important role in the activities like recruitment, promotions, training programmes, performance appraisal, and so on. Making employees aware of their capabilities is very crucial job of these HR professionals, which ultimately leads to the organizational development. He works as a team member and not leader.

Thus the key elements for the success as 'HR professional' is one who would first move 'her / him' and then the company. The role is one of learning, listening and eliciting information rather than one of handling down expertise and teaching.

The HR situation is at a very good stage today where people becoming managers at lower rates. Also both the genders have equal opportunities. Though there are some challenges and stresses to be faced but that is a part of any occupation. HR people deal with these, effectively and above all HR plays a significant role since it deals with men and not machines. It has made itself invaluable to any reasonable sided company without which it is not complete!

HRD is an Emerging Field

Talking to various HRD personnel in Indian organizations, give a hint towards a very important aspect of the human resource management scenario in India, i.e., acceptance. By acceptance we mean, emphasizing the importance of HRD in an organization. The HRD department is still viewed as having secondary importance though it has been gaining tremendous attraction in the call center industry where HRD is described as the 'back-bone' of the organization (Arjun Naik – HRD manager, E-funds).

HRD personnel have also stated other difficulties, as HRD needs to be more proactive with the employees involved. The role of HRD varies from one organization to other but largely involving staffing, personnel selection, roster scheduling, job description, determining pay packets, developing training programs etc.

Overall HRD is still an emerging field in India and needs prioritizing. Even the practices prevalent need to undergo a facelift. (Reshmi Nair, Asst. HR, Shopper Stop).

Case Analysis of HR Managers

Management has been defined by Mary Parker Follett as, 'the art of getting things done through people.' It is clear from this definition that management is concerned with the accomplishment of objectives by utilizing physical and financial resources through the efforts of human resources. Thus, human resource is a crucial sub-system in the process of management.

According to Leon C. Megginson, the term human resources can be thought of as 'the total knowledge, skills creative abilities, talents and aptitudes of an organization's workforce, as well as the value, attitude and beliefs of the individuals involved.'

Human resources play a crucial role in the development process of modern economics. Arthur Lewis observed, 'there are great differences in development between countries, which seems to have roughly equal resources, so it is necessary to inquire into the difference in human behaviour.'

It is often felt that, though the exploitation of natural resources, available of physical and financial resources and international aid play an important role in the growth of modern economics, none of the factors is more significant than efficient and committed manpower. It is in fact said that all development comes from the human mind.

The functions of HRM can be broadly classified into two categories, viz., Managerial functions and operative functions. Managerial functions of HRM involve planning, organizing, directing and controlling. The operative functions of HRM are related to specific activities of HRM, viz., Employment, development, compensation, and relations. All these functions are interacted by managerial functions.

The HR department has staff relations with other departments/managers in the total organization. This department is responsible for advising management from managing director to the lowest line supervisor on all areas relating to the personnel management and industrial relations. This department also performs various functions of employment, training, and development. It represents management in many of the relationships that affect the organization as a whole. It is also responsible for representing various workers problems to management.

The HR department generally acts in an advisory capacity, it provides information, offers suggestions, and is not responsible for the end results. The HR manager must exercise control very tactfully in order to win the confidence and cooperation of all line managers. He has to persuade the line managers to work with staff specialists and not against them.

The authority of the HR manager should derive from concrete personnel policies and programmes and from the advantage and results of accepted specialized knowledge.

As the chief of the HR department, the HR manager has to get effective results with the cooperation of all the employees working in the department and by showing the validity of the concept of team work. The success of this department should be measured in term of its contributions to the personnel programmes.

A survey was conducted of Human Resource Managers from different organizations and their views on the concept of HRD and the problems they face in dealing with the post were recorded. They had to answer a questionnaire relating to their views on HRD and also the stresses and other health problems they have to deal with. The managers were from the age group of 30-50 years of age.

When asked about the nature of their work, they had pretty similar views. Mr. Rajan Mahadik of Oberoi Hotels and Resorts, who is presently the assistant personnel manager, stated that the important functions were employee welfare activities – organizing parties, programmes, annual day, competitions for the employees etc, medical welfare of employee, recruitment and placement, disciplinary actions, rewards and punishment and training.

Mrs. Rekha Shetty, the general manager (HRD) in Bombay Hospital and medical research center stated recruitment, training and development, performance appraisal, employee redressal, exit interviews, job evaluation and description as some of the more important processes in her work process.

Mr. Lyndon D'mello, the personnel manager of Hotel Marine Plaza, stated organizational development, industrial relations, administrative functions, and other general functions as the type of work involved.

According to Mr. Amitabh Dutta, HR involves a lot of administrative work, recruitment and training which are the most important work processes along with performance appraisal.

Mrs. Pranonti Mehta on the other hand stated the same process as mentioned above along with coordinating and maintaining good relationships at each department as well as management and employee relations.

When asked about the challenges and stresses at work as HR manager all replied that conflicts with staff, supervisory problems, interacting with people at different levels in the organization as well as interacting with outside agencies as challenging work. But the most stressful challenging job decided by all was union interference and rivalry.

On the question about how they cope with their challenges and stress in the work situation they replied that they exercised. Mr. Rajan Mahadik said that the personal development programmes give him insight and help him deal with his problems. Mrs. Rekha Shetty said that she goes on a weekend detoxification where she leaves all her work behind and engage in some light hobbies like reading or swimming so that she is relaxed during the weekend to confront the coming week. Many managers also reported using relaxation techniques doing meditation and yoga otherwise they found their job very interesting and the challenges even more attractive.

About their perceptions of HRD in organizations everyone agreed that human resources were the most important element of an organization and hence the HRD which caters to this important element is to extreme importance for the proper functioning of an organization. However, according to Mr. Hyndon D'mello, the term 'Human Resource Department' is old wine in a new bottle'. He state that looking after the human resources of an organization was given importance previously by the management the same thing is taking place now but under the new term of 'HRD' Mr. Rajan Mahadile views employees as internal guest and they have to be treated well to get good results. However, the HR manager is also like an internal police dealing with rules and regulations in the organization and coordination of staff and management. HRD scenario as a whole is a very important department, Human Resource Management has come a long way and as long as companies keep stressing the importance of people then there will always be a job for human resource managers.

On the topic of health problems suffered by these managers, they stated stress: physical as well as mental as the main problem.

However, it was not too much that they could not deal with it. According to them this small stress was of little importance as they enjoyed their jobs and found their work very interesting. A few of them experienced backaches, headaches, body pain, loss of appetite, etc. A few did have problems sleeping and also staying awake.

According to their replies to the health questionnaire all the respondents denied suffering from any problems related to fatigue, breaching, nervousness, eating problems, sleeping or high blood pressure. None of the respondents smoked. One problem which all of them had some trouble with was aches in the neck and upper and lower back. This they attributed to the long hours they spent sitting in their chairs. However, they namely had pains of this kind. They loved the challenges that came with their job and not have any kinds of complaints about the effect of their work on their health.

A human resource department is important for every organization for recruitment, marketing, and management. The nature of their job involves – training, recruitment, staff and leadership development, performance appraisal, interpretation, and application of laws, rules, policies and procedures, and other personnel services. It is also the agency that deals with employee grievances and labour or union trouble. It provides scope for development and advancement of employees through hailing development etc. Thus it causes the development of various sources of human resources to meet the organizational needs.

The HR Woman Manager

"I am very satisfied with whatever I have achieved. Being an employee and being manager differs from each other in many ways. Being a good manager you have to adapt yourself with different people having different attitudes. It teaches you to develop yourself, also importance of time. As a manager you are responsible to your institution, so careful and effective decision making is essential aspect." – a woman manager

The female managers perceive themselves as well-established in their fields and their work processes mainly involve organizational development, recruitment policies, training, interviews, and performance appraisals. The challenges and stresses they face center around workplace, competition, long working hours, dealing with different people, selecting the right candidates etc. all of them felt that HRD is an integral part for any organization. To sum up, we can say that people's issues are taking an elevated role in the strategic business decisions and organizational management and HRD is growing more and more as people realize its importance for the survival in any organization.

"Being a lady police inspector, I feel that males have dominated this field from earlier time. Now females are also actively participating providing valuable contribution. My career as Police Inspector is delightful experience for me, since through my service I am getting opportunity to serve my country and reform my society which otherwise is not possible. I am trying my level best to achieve my goal."

The First-line Manager

Individual and group supervision is important parts of the first-line manager's job as a manager of practice. However, managing practice involves more than formal supervision, as it looks at the best use of the whole team's resources. This means that the first line manager should know what staff are doing and how they are doing it and be able to give consistent, judicious leadership to the team. Supervision is often thought of as a one-to-one activity. However, many of the principles and aims of individual supervision can be applied to group supervision. If you supervise a group of colleagues you are likely to find some of the skills and techniques of team development useful. The difference between the two is probably one of emphasis: group supervision is likely to focus more on direct work with service users and careers, looking at the inter-personal skills, judgements and approaches used by group members. In supporting and leading the professional work of your team, you are likely to use all three approaches: the table below sets out some of their characteristics to help you decide which approach to use when. A mixture of all three will probably be most effective. For example, a statutory team used to thinking in terms of individual allocated cases may find group supervision very helpful. A day care team, used to collective direct work may find the change of emphasis provided by a team development session just as stimulating.

In the conclusion it can be said that future has many challenges for the managers of tomorrow. The most important challenge is how personnel executive and his staff can help in improving organizational effectiveness; and how best he can utilize the results of behavioural scientists for the benefit of the people at work. One part of the challenge lies in how to create and manage the various personnel sub-systems in a way compatible with the thrust toward more participative, result-oriented, adaptive, and humanistic organizations. Systems of job design, staffing, appraisal compensation, collective bargaining, organizational justice and training and development must all be examined and improved toward these ends.

Human Resources Redefined

Human resources can be defined as the total knowledge, skills, creative ability talents and aptitudes obtained in the population, whereas from new point of the individual enterprise, they represent the total of the inherent abilities, acquired knowledge and skills are exemplified in the talents and aptitude of its employees.

The human factors to a whole consisting of interrelated, interdependent and interacting physiological, psychological, sociological and ethical components.

With regard to the nature of work/process involves HRM is concerned with improving contributions of people towards the effectiveness of the organizations. Their contributions can be assessed in terms of specific personnel/human resource outcomes, attraction, performance, attendance, and satisfaction.

Any new assignment is a challenge but the biggest challenge faced by the HR managers is getting the right candidate in a short span of time and meeting deadlines.

Everybody has a different way of meeting deadlines. Most of HR managers feel that they need to get on with their work, be open to new ideas, and meet their deadlines. Some found a solution in talking it out colleagues/ friends or spending time with family.

Perception of the HRD scenario is extremely positive. It is being viewed as a fast expanding field and also very promising. It is seen as a critical department, which could does wonders to the company.

The human resources are assuming increasing significance in modern organization. Obviously, a majority of the problems in organizations setting are human and social rather than physical, technical or economic. The failure to recognize this fact causes immense loss to the nation, enterprise, and the individual.

The work profile of HRM includes right from selection of employees to maintaining these employees for long term and also to provide them training and appraising their performance. According to a manager, "the job of HRM is to run the organization."

HR managers have to do a lot of research and study and like all the managers have to keep pace with the ever-growing world changing times. It requires a lot of effort and back breaking effort on the part of the manager. Rested upon them is the greatest responsibility of managing manpower.

Such an effort on part involves both mental and physical stress. Stress becomes a part of our life and this manager hardly think of stressors as a challenge in their work. HR managers have accepted such stressful life and they have adjusted to it that they hardly have to think of coping mechanism. In other words coping with stress has become very automatic and mechanized. One of the coping techniques used in the organization was going out for movie on weekend to relax oneself. A manager said, "we don't really care for stress unless it is a grave one."

Health problems are not many, also not to be different from their colleagues from other departments. When asked, everybody answered by saying that health problems has nothing to do with the department they work for but completely depends of person to person.

Larsen & Toubro Ltd. was the first company in India to introduce the HRD concept in 1975 with an objective to facilitate growth of employees. A paradigm shift could be visualized with a human perspective rather production oriented.

Today the HR managers will have to get up from their tables and move closer to the employees and the business. They have to understand and assimilate, deploy all their tools such as training and development etc. to achieve the needs of the organization, and explain these to the top management, monitor and derive results. HR managers thus have an extremely important role to play in formulating and implementing business strategy as it adds value to the most important resource of organizations namely human resources.

Summary

The functions of HR managers include activities like recruitment and selection, orientation and placement, performance management, manpower planning, corporate training, improvement management, communications, welfare, safety and health. The most important quality of a HR manager is to deal successfully with people. Their stresses as HR managers are time management, work pressures, retaining the talented workforce, improving work cultures, etc. The HR managers have developed stress management skills to keep themselves fit. Most of the HR managers felt that they did not have any physical health problems due to work pressure. The kind of health problems they had due to work were acidity, headaches and tiredness. Major health hazards amongst HRD personnel are related to long working hours. The managers reported hypertension and blood pressure problems.

The HR professionals have moved up to the higher echelons in the organizations. HR managers play a crucial role in framing business strategies. Hence, they must be aware of business policies and the way other areas of organization function. They need business orientations and perspectives. They have to understand the realities of the business as the HRD policies presently are being integrated into the overall policies of the organization.

The challenge of HR department is to perform for the growth of their human resources for the development of the organization. Satisfaction of employees is the responsibility of HR managers. To achieve connectivity in the organization is the great challenge in HR manager's life. HR managers usually have hectic schedules and just work for the human resource of their organization.

The HRD field is a rising. Human resources play a crucial role in the business development. HRD is an integral part of any organization. The human resources are assuming increasing significance in organizations. A woman manager expresses "The HR situation is at a very good stage today. HR plays a significant role since it deals with men and not machines." The female managers perceive themselves established in their organization.

6
Women Managers

Working women compose a large proportion of the workforce today. Interestingly the attitude of society towards working women is also rapidly changing. There is a definite difference between male and female manager as well as between women manager and women who are not working. For women to be working as manager is really a challenge to them in India. This chapter discusses the stress and health aspect of women managers, and how they cope up with work challenges? Though the women managers experience obstacles in their careers, they have positive perception of their future career in the corporate management. They have a strong need for growth. They sometimes feel more subject to external control. To succeed in management, women offer greater intrinsic motivation. Action plan and programmes to reduce stress and health related problems for women managers and suggested.

Introduction

The new concept of 'management' as we see today was established in the late 19th century when the organizations required such a specialization. Women's participation in management came such later due to increased education and liberation movement among women. Though women today represent around 50 per cent of the world population, they are far away to half of the corporate manager. In the later part of 1970's women managers have become increasingly visible. In the management profession, they are largely in lower level, to a better extent in middle level and only 5 per cent in upper management.

The literature review on women managers includes several studies regarding the issues as follows; the attitudes and perception of women managers towards their family, occupation, working women as well as gender related issues. The behaviour that gets them the coveted promotion and what do the man think about their female boss? How large a role does their family play? What are the issues that they lose their sleep over? Are women better bosses and colleagues for women than men? What is special about the women who make it the top? What are the qualities that female executive display? The issues that broadly emerged in research studies are as follow:

Issues Considered on Women Managers

- Dual roles
- Executive couples
- Job satisfaction
- Sexual harassment
- Conditions of work
- Recruitment and promotion
- Career aspirations
- Performance
- Discrimination in salaries
- Career planning and counseling
- Career success
- Gender differences
- Power and related issues
- Sex role stereotypes

As the above mentioned issues indicate, there are no studies conducted on stress and health of the women managers. Hence this chapter attempts to explore various stresses and health problems that the women managers face and the ways in which they cope up with the work challenges.

The chapter has been presented in the following themes:

- Stresses of women managers

- Women managers and their health problems
- How women managers cope up with work challenges?
- Specific cases of stress and coping
- Message to the young women managers

Stresses of Women Managers

The chief barriers that retard women's progress in management include stereotypical perceptions of women's abilities and qualifications, traditional attitudes towards women's family roles, and broadly the discrimination against women.

The stresses experienced by women managers at workplace varied, depending upon the nature and type of work that they did. In general, meeting deadlines, getting the work done from various people, lack of support from others and handling different types of clients were perceived to be the major stresses at their workplace.

The stresses experienced at different levels are different. Most of the women managers reported their major stress as meeting deadlines, which includes lots of responsibilities and perfection in work. Other main stressors and challenges are dealing with people and managing them, long working hours, competition, keeping up with latest technology. The women executives observe the internal politics between colleagues stressful. An important additional stress factor for many women at any level is the delicate juggling act that they have to perform between work and other responsibilities. Despite work pressures, women remain the primary caretakers in the family front.

The Major Stresses of Women Managers

- Getting the work done by their subordinates
- Clashes with superiors
- Competition
- Dual responsibilities of household and job
- Meeting deadlines
- Lack of support from others
- Handling different types of clients

- Long working hours
- Keeping up with latest technology
- Internal politics between colleagues

When asked about their major stress or challenges, a woman manager said "it was to meet the stringent deadlines and keep the team motivated". Another felt "as if she had to constantly prove herself. I felt torn between the household and office work."

Women Managers and Their Health Problems

The women at the management level had to work harder and also face tough competition from their male colleagues. Some of them felt that job bias against women who wanted to move up in the management ladder existed. Most of them did not have any sort of health problems due to work pressures. Some health problems experienced by women managers were headaches, exhaustion, gastric problems, low appetite, asthma, low blood pressure, and sleeplessness. The younger age group (with lesser work experience) has less health problems due to work pressure.

Health problems that women managers face

- Headaches, migraines
- Back pains
- Exhaustion
- Gastric problems, less hunger
- Asthma
- Low blood pressure
- Sleeplessness

How Women Manager Cope up with Work Challenges

Different individuals have different ways of coping with stresses. The coping strategies used by the women managers are time management, yoga, meditation, exercises, and also planning the work properly so that there are fewer problems.

The way managers cope with stresses depend upon which phase of career they are. In the early phase, since they couldn't afford to take holidays, they would overcome the challenges by positive thinking, staying energetic and gathering more experience. But in the middle and late phase of the career it was seen that they could take holidays and also do exercises. The overall perceptions of being a woman manager at all the phases were highly satisfactory besides the fact of being financially independent.

The coping strategies, vary from person to person, among the most common are, to do something other than the job-related work and take a break from routine. Others are gathering emotional support, finishing of work at right time, work hard since the beginning, improving communications etc. Listening to music and talking about the problems to others also helped.

The overall perceptions show that most women managers were happy to be working and their jobs give them a lot of satisfaction. Some felt that they could have achieved more if others did not restrict them. Some others felt that they put all their time in work and their family felt neglected.

To cope up with these stresses and challenges these women managers try to get the full cooperation of their subordinates and they keep good terms with their superiors. All of them have mentioned that they perceive themselves as a "successful manager." According to them the job they are doing is very challenging and responsible that requires thorough knowledge, high self-confidence and in-depth understanding of the situations.

The ways Women Managers cope up with work challenges

- Discussing it with friends and colleagues.
- Occupy themselves with activities disconnected with work.
- Speak out work problems with spouse.
- Spending time on one's own.
- Practice Yoga
- Prayer to overcome stress.
- Completing the task that is causing the stress.

Some Specific Cases of Stress and Coping

- **E-business women:** the major stresses reported by women managers engaged in E-business included shift work, meeting deadlines, co-ordination between team members, and maintaining a balance between work and family. Women also showed some health problems like fatigue, stress and weight loss. Most of the managers perceive their career as a long journey of hard work and dedication. They also believe that it is a very challenging and responsible position. They emphasize on values like honesty and dedication to reach the top. However it was seen that most of the women work actively towards eliminating stress by meditating, taking break and exercising.
- **The bank women managers:** the women managers in the bank had difficulty dealing with customers. They reported that it is irritating to handle them. They were competent of long hours of work. There was a loss of weight, after joining bank work as a woman manager reported. They have headaches due to work tension and one also says that there is lack of appetite. The married women managers have to manage work at office as well as home, so it is tiring for them. They tend to transfer 'home tensions' at work and 'work tensions' at home. All of them follow different types of coping strategies, some like to relax and sleep, while others holiday, watch TV, swim, and some work systematically so that the work becomes enjoyable and tension is avoided. Almost all women managers in the bank are very happy with their progress. Only some of them reported that they find it irritating, when compared with male counterparts. All of them perceive their career to be satisfying and are happy with perks available.
- **School principals**: When these women were asked about major stresses and challenges at workplace, the answers varied from recruiting teachers in the school, introducing various exams, handling administrative work, maintaining public relations, and dealing with staff members inclined to shirk from their duty. When asked how does this affect

their family life, the general response was that over a period of 18-20 years of service, the family members seem to have accepted the fact that the lady has to work, for her own needs and satisfaction and hence they also have given a helping hand. The various health problems faced by these women include high blood pressure due to workload, acidity, headaches, and anxiety. The coping techniques used mainly are having positive approach toward work and life, use of relaxing techniques like reading, listening to music etc. Acceptance of the problem was also a way in which one of women managers handle the situation. According to her one may not succeed in every examination for promotion, but denial of the fact leads to further problems. In fact, acceptance of the failure itself helps and then the use of positive approach helps to come out of the situation.

Message to the Young Women Managers

Based on their experience, the women managers gave messages to the young managers. The most common messages were, learn from experience, positive thinking, constant generation of self-motivation and the most important one is to have time for alternative activities or entertainment. The other messages to young managers included, knowing their priorities and being balanced, being confident, working hard, being honest, learning to manage people, being flexible, being focused and making decisions.

The women managers stressed on this fact that absolute and complete knowledge of what the job entails is necessary. This could be by discussing it with others at a similar level or your superior and reading up on materials available. Along with knowledge, it is equally important to be able to handle people around you and working below you, and develop and maintain interpersonal relationships in the work place.

The message of women managers to young managers is to be positive, devoted, committed, practical, and sincere. Put in your best efforts. Sincere commitment in your job is very important, regardless of the type of job. Most of them placed a lot of emphasis on hard work and dedication. They felt that all women should be independent and must keep a proper balance between work and family life. According to a woman manager, "to sum up, it is being confident, sincere and understanding to be a successful manager."

Conclusions

Management is no more a domain only for men: From the literature review and survey observations, it is understood that the number of women in management has increased in recent years but there are lots of factors which influence their role as women managers. Traditionally women throughout the world have been assigned lower positions than that of men. But now, with the rapid economic, technological and social change, women are being presented with unique opportunities to enrich their working lives. Hence, management is no more a domain only for men. She is out of the closet and raring to go. Consequently women are also changing their own perceptions and taking up new career options. At the workplace they are at war with the traditional image given by the male dominated society and constantly endeavoring to prove one step above men if not keeping pace with them. Also additional responsibilities of home increase their stress. But that does not deter them from pursuing the ultimate goal. Though married women face more stress because balancing a family and doing well at workplace, being born homemakers, they are balancing both the worlds gracefully. Gone are the days of women managers who had to make painful decision to choose between home and career and consequently had to remain single. More and more married women managers are coming to the fore and making success of it now.

Perceptions of women managers: The women managers' perceptions about their careers range from positive to negative. They are committed to their jobs and enjoy positions of responsibility. Though there are no conspicuous promotion policies separately for men and women, time constraints and family responsibility do hamper their promotions. They are bound to face problems in relationships with male subordinates but that does not affect their productivity. Women have superior integrity, which many a time lands them to handle very sensitive positions and issues. The new age women have rightly understood the male psyche and they are constantly making efforts to better the performance. Most of them perceived their career as a manager as satisfactory but ever ready for newer challenges. The woman manager has a load of responsibilities and is prepared to accept more. As she is not used to manipulation, unhealthy competition, and politics in the organization corrupts the environment and this becomes a major cause of stress for her. However, the women managers have good opportunities in the job and they see themselves growing. All the women managers are not facing health problems. With their pleasant nature they make the workplace very congenial. The motherly nature present in every woman makes her a good counselor clubbed with the positive attitude towards work, she turns the workplace enjoyable and worth coming back to.

Women managers loved their jobs and felt important: The women managers' perceived their careers very well. In her perception only a very thin line separates career from home. She applies the same devotion and personal care to her career, which she gives to her family. Their responses about their jobs included meticulous planning, challenging, confidence, satisfaction, immense value, independence, empowerment, and internal locus of control. This indicates that women see their careers as very important point of life. One of the observations was that women were very enthusiastic about their career, loved doing their jobs, elated at the importance and the status it gave them. Pregnancy is no more a threat to them. She in fact liked working till she had to take leave. Women managers display a lot of competence and skill and is a growing community that is adding greatly to the productive working population of India.

The women managers are proud of what they are doing but felt that they had to balance between their office and family life. For this, they had to make a few sacrifices, which they are willing to do, so long as their work is appreciated. This is the same attitude that most women managers in society have but our effort should be that we can shed the condescending attitude we have towards them and make women proud of their work and make the family atmosphere such that women feel good about their contributions.

Optimistic about careers: Women managers see themselves as more sociably fulfilled and are very optimistic about their careers. Sometimes during certain situations they feel really tense. It appears that they have generally healthier self-image. But sometimes she feels that her wings are clipped in comparison with men but that does not force her to compromise. She does not loose sight of her goal, is quick in adapting new methods to improve her performance. Women managers are more interested in having friendly congenial colleagues and work-challenges where their individual accomplishment is appreciated and they get opportunities to be creative. They have a strong need for growth. Managerial career is highly volatile. It becomes necessary for them to overcome a variety of general gender specific obstacles in our culture in order to pursue their managerial career especially for women with family. Nowadays these women are getting good support, especially motivation from their families. A flexible attitude of life partners is also brings important relief for them.

Sexual exploitation: As we already know working women are faced with the problem of sexual exploitation. However, it happens not only with women working in lower jobs but also to women on managerial positions. Women have to constantly take care of themselves in order to prevent sexual exploitation. Though certain enabling provisions have been introduced to arm women in fighting this social disease, she is still at a disadvantage and is fighting the age old image that women are for pleasure and not for purpose. Very little has been done to improve their lot. In seeking justice for the damage done to her, many a time she earns the wrath of the management and has to sacrifice her claim to a better career.

Cooperation from their subordinates: The major stress of women at managerial positions is dealing with people of various backgrounds. Most of them come across uncooperative subordinates but cooperative bosses and vice versa. Women managers from all fields do face many problems related to gender differences. Women are taking up these challenging issues with lot of courage and are able to overcome these issues. Most of them are well established carrying out their roles efficiently. It is becoming very clear that an organization having a neutral policy towards its male and female managers would be successful in achieving its goals without any hurdles.

Undertake stress prevention programs: Women managers in Indian organizations experience a great deal of stress, which can later lead to anxiety, depression and de-motivation. In fact, many organizations are undertaking prevention programs to help reduce stress among executives. Women are born stress busters. With a little helping attitude from the organization she serves, she easily overcomes this difficulty and copes with stress better than man do and work her way to success.

Upgrade skills: The managerial career of a women may look like a clear and straight but path are complex. The rate of environmental change is also placing imperative demands on organization for survival and prosperity. So for the women managers are concerned, there is a constant pressure to update their skill and knowledge and to retain their status in organization. Woman is a home maker and as far as possible she would try to keep the family together. Now, women are no more shy of environmental changes as there is a paradigm shift in her attitude towards her career as she is starting to believe in the theory of career for career sake.

Intrinsic motivation: As women managers are partners in dual career families, their incomes are not the sole means of support for their famlies. So material rewards are relatively of less importance to them. But it is rewarding to her that the combined income enables a better life style. They are enjoying their vital position and are accepting their responsibilities. To succeed in management, women offer greater intrinsic motivation.

Effective coping: As today's world is changing drastically, industrialization and modernization along with their desirable effects has brought occupational disease. Stress is a recognized killer and a major contributor to workplace illness. Backaches, headaches, blood pressure, acidity, vision related problems due to frequent exposure to computers are imposing health threats on women managers. Many women managers feel stressed out due to work pressure, too much expectations, and multiple role-playing. Sometimes it becomes very difficult to cope. Self-management and disciplined approach to her career helps her to overcome stress. Effective coping styles or patterns in responding to various stressful situations help. They used task oriented coping strategies that include better time scheduling, adjustment of priorities, and determining course of action. Some of them prefer yoga and meditation to cope with stress. They look to their organization for relief and understanding. They are very happy, satisfied with their careers and are aspiring to achieve more and more and are ready to overcome obstacles. The women managers emphasized on the importance of effective team building as they agree that without harmonious relations with subordinates it is impossible to achieve.

Interaction with co-workers or customers: Women managers seem to be exceptionally good with interactions of a one to one nature with co-workers or customers. The temperament of women managers is a good predictor of the reaction they have towards stress on the job. When in need, they play the role of counselors and are able to extract better productivity from their subordinates as also building up the image of their organization.

Women are more successful in performance of their job-related tasks along with their efficiency in personal relations. There is definitely an impact of different social setting at the work place.

Advice to young managers: The women managers are trying to be more and more attentive in this world of rapid change. They advise young managers to be flexible, adjust to new changes, be motivated, be competitive, and be innovative. They have specifically pointed out the importance of time and learning new things for young managers to keep pace with the changing world.

Development of self and career: More and more women are actively participating and also have occupied vital positions in leading institutions in India. They contribute uniquely to the organizations. Beside constant on-the-job training, self-development, improved self-image, cooperation from the family and society at large are very necessary for their healthy development of career. They are serving as role models for others while achieving successfully. It is rightly quoted 'when you educate a man you educate a person but when you educate a woman you educate whole generation.'

A new woman manager: Despite the increasing number of women being appointed to executive or managerial posts, they still face fundamental problems in getting through and staying there. These problems are partly because of men's difficulties in adjusting to the idea of female bosses and the corresponding problems the women managers have in adjusting to a superior role. Reaching the top is akin to winning a battle. Many women expressed the glass-ceiling syndrome. Women in top executive positions are rare. This is because married women at their twilight years, even after reaching certain level in the hierarchy, are reluctant to carry on with the career once her spouse retires from active service. Although more and more have managerial positions, invisible barrier still prevent most from climbing to the highest corporate levels.

Women executives have possessed a high level of achievement motivation and being close to type A behaviour. They also face the problems of role overload, role isolation, role expectation, fear of poor performance and inter role distance. Senior executives are high on task orientation and they deliver the goods within a short period. They possess generator style orientation of creative problem solving. The role of new woman manager is more challenging and rewarding.

She is expected to perform efficiently as a homemaker as well as efficient manager in the competitive world. Today with feminist movement, all round development of women is in the focus. She is juggling her roles remarkably well, leaving the imprint of her caliber wherever she is.

Achievements of remarkable women have reached great heights! Although some amount of stress level is present, they didn't allow this stress to interfere with their professional lives and found effective means of coping with them. Through a combination of luck, power, judgment, planning, and strength, women in management stand their way through all obstacles. They have realized their inner strength with which they face the challenging circumstances. Success does not come easily to them as they are confronting a society steeped in age-old traditions and make beliefs. Coping with all the stresses both physical as well as psychological, quietly demanding recognition of their mettle, the women managers of today have eroded the male bastion. They are proving that they are a formidable force to be reckoned with and it is no more a male dominated society. It is better that the society gracefully recognizes her due share and role for a better tomorrow.

Recommeded Action Plan

Organizations and employers that hire women managers need to take action in order to reduce their stresses and related health threats by introducing suitable techniques. Some action plans and programmes are suggested below:

- Besides, changing roles in family, sharing responsibilities, flexible work timings and childcare facilities, major steps have to be taken to get equal opportunities for women managers. These also include stringent rules against sex discrimination. There is a need to develop policies on matters as equal opportunity, sexual harassment, and the special occupational, health, and safety needs of women.
- Constant refresher training on the job is very essential and should be imparted at specific intervals, depending on the need of the woman manager.
- Health counselling by the trained occupational health psychologists will be useful. Full-time / part-time or visiting

medical doctor / Psychiatrist / Psychologist is a must in organizations.

- Interruptions to a woman's career pathway are cited as one of the major causes of women's lower status and salaries in management. Career planning and counseling is another important tool for both women and men to "get ahead" and to provide an advantage in the competitive managerial world.
- Employee Assistance Programmes (EAP) are required to seek professional help on personal, educational and vocational development of children. Pepsi Co. has a "concierge service" which helps employees with tasks that need to be done during workday (e.g., lining up a baby sitter, contracting for house repairs).
- Humor room at the work place helps in improving emotional health. Eastman Kodak has a "humor room" where employees can read light, funny materials or engage in activities to take their mind off a stressful day. Ben and Jerry's has a "Joy Gang" charged with creating happiness in the workplace. This group plans birthdays and anniversary celebrations and creates other joyful events.
- Other programmes and activities are very important in reducing and preventing stress on the part of the women executives as follows. Creches at workplace, Flextime, compressed working week, Orientation on Gender-sensitivity and sexual harassment from men at workplace, periodical medical examinations, Yoga for improved physical and mental health, Tele-commuting: receiving / sending work between home and office.
- Three prescriptions for women managers: When work and family pressures are extremely stressful, never "add on" to your work. While prioritizing and compartmentalizing between work and family, listen to your inner voice and make your own judgement. Continuous stressful working will definitely affect your health, observe daily relaxation, breathing exercises.

Researchers are of the view that some innovative work-family programs for women managers decrease family conflict, job dissatisfaction, and stress-related problems. These are as follows: Child or eldercare benefits: these include children's facilities at work site and transportation of aging parents. Convenience Benefits: this refers to onsite services such as dry cleaning, ATM machines, postal services. Health promotion Benefits: include fitness centers, health screenings, stress management clinics. But it is difficult to empirically demonstrate whether these programs have direct positive impact on one's performance.

References

1. Agarawal K.G. Female Executives in Government Systems, *Social Change,* Vol. 20 (2), 32-40, June 1990.
2. Arya Rashmi, *Women in Public Sector,* Madak Publication Pvt. Ltd., Bombay 1990.
3. Buddhapriya Sangamitra and Khandelwal Preeta, Sex Role Stereotyped and Women Managers A Reality, *Indian Journal of Industrial Research,* Vol. 31 (1), 72-90, 1995.
4. Carmen Luck, Women in Higher Education Management in Thailand, *Asian Journal of Women's Studies,* Vol. 3 (4), 51-57, 1997.
5. Commea T.K. Family in Transition Pattern of Response to Change, *Times of India,* Bombay, Dec. 17, 1994.
6. *Indian Express,* U.S. Woman Executive Are Advancing. 11th February, 1997.
7. Irene H. Frieze, Josephine Olson and Deborah Cain Good, Perceived and Actual Discrimination In the Salaries of Male and Female Managers, *Journal of Applied Social Psychology,* Vol. 20 (1), 46-47, 1990.
8. Joshi Rama J., Women in Management-Perception and Attitude of Mangers, *Indian Journal of Industrial Relations.* Vol. 26 (2), 213-221, 1990.
9. Kaila H.L. How do Metro Managers Cope With Their Stresses, And Health Problems? *The Journal of Health Management,* 5, 1, 139-144,1 2003.

10. Kaila H.L. 'Heavy Duty Stress', *The Indian Express, Headstar*, Vol. 4, Issue 30, 12, Mumbai, July 4, 2002.

11. Kaila H.L., Attitude and Perception of Female Executives towards Various Issues—A Psychological Analysis, *Journal of Community Guidance and Research*, Vol. 16., Issue 16, No. 2, pp. 121-139, 1999.

12. Kalbagh Chetna: *Women's Development: Women In Enterprise And Profession*. Discovery Publishing House, New Delhi, 1991.

13. Kapur Promilla, *Marriage And The Working Women In India*. Vikas Publications, Delhi, 1970.

14. Kapur Promilla, *The Changing Status Of The Working Women In India*, Vikas Publishing House Pvt. Ltd., Bombay, 1974.

15. Kapur Promilla, *Women Administration in India*, Vikas Publications, Bombay, 1990.

16. Kraisonwadi Napasri, *Women Executive, A Sociological Study In The Role Effectiveness*, Rawat Publications, Jaipur, 1989.

17. Mahajan Amarjit, Women's Two Roles: *A Study of Role Conflict. Indian Journal of Social Work*, Vol. 26, No. 4, 173-183, Jan 1966.

18. Mandal Osmita, Women Executives—Power and Related Issues, *Indian Journal of Social Work*, Vol. 55 (4), 71-81, 1994.

19. Mehta Shefali, *Self-Actualization among Professional Working Women*, SNDT Women's University, Mumbai, 1993.

20. Melamed Turia, Career Success: An Assessment of A Gender—Specific Model, *Journal of Occupational and Organisational Psychology*. Vol. 69, No. 4; 217- 242, 1996.

21. Mitra S. Male Executives More Stress-Prone Than Females: Study. *Everyman's Science*, Vol. 31 (6), 40-45, 1997.

22. Panchanatham N. And Karuppiah K. R. K. A Study Of Executive Leadership Styles And Problem Solving Behaviour, *Indian Journal of Industrial Relations*, Vol. 29, No. 1, 101-107, July 1993.

23. Parikh Indira J and Shah N.A. Woman Managers in Transition: From Homes to Corporate Office. *Indian Journal of Social Work*, Vol. LV, No.2, 161-172, April 1994.

24. Patrice Rosenthal, David Guest And Ricardo Peccei, Gender Differences In Manager's Causal Explanation For Their Work Performance: A Study In Two Organizations, *Journal of Occupational and Organizational Psychology*, Vol. 69, 145-151, 1996.

25. Rajagopal T.S. *Indian Women In The New Age,* Jaya Publishers, Mysore 1936.

26. Rao V.N. And Parthasarathy R. Stress And Strain of Executives: Implications for Mental Health Approach, *Indian Journal of Occupational Health,* Vol. 39 (3), 171 -176, 1996.

27. Reddy, Raghunandha C, *Changing Status Of Educated Working Women,* B.R. Publications Corp, Delhi, 1986.

28. Rohatgi Sushila; Woman Executives and The Social Scenario, *Indian Management,* Vol. 71, (2), 81-86, April 1988.

29. Sastry Nalini, Woman Employees: An Emerging Issue Of HRM In Organisations; Department Of Humanities & Social Sciences; Indian Institute Of Technology, Bombay. 1998 (unpublished report).

30. Satish Pai, S. Ravishankar, Dhar U. and B. Pattanayak. *Human Resource Development Skills for Organizational Excellence.* Mumbai, Himalaya Publishing House. 1999.

31. Sekaran Uma ; Is Career More Salient For Men Than Woman: An Empirical Investigation; *Indian Journal of Applied Psychology,* Vol. 21 (1), 33-39, 1984.

32. Singh Coomi, *A Study of Women Executives in Bombay: Their Roles at Home and At Work.* SNDT Women's University, Bombay 1990.

33. Singh H.K.And Singh.Meera, Frontiers of General Management. New Delhi: Kanishka Publishers, 1998.

34. The Bombay Times. 'Tight Deadlines Make City Managers Sweat', Mumbai, June 26, 2002.

35. *The Economic Times,* Sunday, State of the World's Woman Report, July 14, 1985.

36. Unwalla Jerro M, A Study Of Woman Executives At Work And At Home, *Indian Dissertation Abstract* 17 (3), 383, July-Sept 1988.

Appendix

HR managers interviewed from different organizations

1. Kodak India ltd.
2. Personnel Search Services Pvt. ltd.
3. Siemens India
4. Transworld group
5. Schenectady Herdillia ltd.
6. BASF India LTD.
7. HCL technologies Mumbai Ltd.
8. SYNTEL Ltd. (computer technological Institute)
9. Fortune Financial Services (India) Ltd.
10. PROFILE
11. KANKE
12. COLLIERS
13. Future Finance Services India Ltd.
14. Pidilite chemicals
15. Godrej & Boyce
16. Goa Marriott resort
17. Goa Telecom
18. Dempo – V.S.Dempo & Co. Pvt. Ltd.
19. Geno Pharmaceuticals
20. Hi-Tech
21. J.P. & Morgan-Chase
22. World Network Services
23. Hotel President

24. Aviation Industry
25. Tata shares
26. L & T (Engg. Unit)
27. Ma foe consultancy
28. L & T finance LTD
29. Siemens
30. Castors
31. McDonalds
32. Cadburys
33. HDFC
34. Sodexo Coupons
35. Shoppers Shop LTD
36. SCMS
37. E-funds International
38. Milkyway communication
39. Oberoi Hotels and Resorts
40. Bombay Hospital and Medical research Center
41. Wacker Matriarch Chemicals Pvt. LTD
42. Disha Travel
43. Hotel Marine Plaza
44. Oberoi Hotels and Resorts
45. CMC Pvt. Ltd.
46. Aggreko (Dubai)
47. Omni Consultancy Services
48. Kamla Group Pvt. Ltd.
49. OSMC Pvt. Ltd.
50. M.B.T. (Mahindra British telecom)
51. ICIC Bank (Mahalakshmi)
52. Spides systems PVT Ltd.
53. STAR India

54. Covansys India Pvt. Ltd.
55. Hindustan Coco Cola Marketing
56. Rallis India Ltd.
57. Ocwen Financial Solutions Private Ltd. Bangalore
58. Mainstream training HRD center
59. Siemens Information system LTD
60. P.Games Private Limited
61. Tata Engineering
62. Development Credit Bank
63. Hari Paul & Prakash Associates
64. Union Bank of India
65. Godrej Industries Ltd.
66. Raymonds
67. Mahindra & Mahindra
68. J. Virji Traders
69. K.G. N Agency
70. Mahtre Co. Ltd
71. Panjwani Petro Pvt. Ltd
72. Saru Petrochemical Pvt. Ltd.

Bibilography

Akhilesh K.B. and R. Sekar (2000). Personnel HR Profession in India: Selected Results of A National Survey. In: HRM 2000: Indian Perspectives Pune: NIPM.

Arthur Young, (1986) The Manager's Handbook. The Practical Guide to Successful Management. London: Sphere Books Ltd.

Atkin and Gibbler (1987). Varieties of Managerial Learning, Psychological Abstracts, Vol. 16 (2), Page 36-48.

Aswapthappa K. (1997). Human Resources and Personnel Management. New Delhi: Tata Mc Graw Hill Publishing Company Ltd.

Beltom Trevor (2001). An Introduction to Human Resource Management. New Delhi: A Maya Black Well Imprint. pp. 1-10, 21-25.

Bhardwaj Gopa and Rajneesh Sharma (1990). Human Relations and Organizational Climate: An Empirical Analysis, Indian Journal of Industrial Relations, April 1990, Vol. 28, No 1, pp. 393-399.

Blake R and Mouton J. (1996). The New Managerial Grid. Mumbai: Jaico Publishing house. Sixth edition.

Braham, J. (1994). Human Resource Planning. Institute of Personnel and Development, p. 187-195

Carlotta Jacobson (2002). Social entrepreneurs. *www.fastcompany.com/fast50_02/profile/jacobson370*

Chatterjee Bhaskar (1995). Human Resource Management - A Contemporary Text. Mumbai: Sterling Publishers Pvt. Ltd. p. 54.

Christopher Orpen (1993). The Multifactorial Achievement Scale As A Predictor of Salary Growth and Motivation Among Middle Managers, Psychological Studies, Vol. 38, No 2, p. 79-81.

Das Hari and Manimala M. J. (1993). Roles Indian Managers Play: An Investigation Into The Nature of Managerial Work In India, October 1993, Indian Journal of Industrial Relations, Vol. 29, No 2, pp. 133-150.

Dhingra O.P, and Pathak V.K. (1972). Professional Background of The Indian Personnel Managers, (Aug-Oct), PACT, 11-17.

Douglas Jackson N, Paunonen, Sampo V, and Rothstein Mitchell G. (1987). Personality, Vocational Interests and Job Satisfaction, 1987 (Sept), Journal of Employment Counseling, Vol. 24 (3), p. 82-96.

Drucker Peter F. 1986. The Practice of Management, pp. 2-10. Illinois: Harper Business..

Dwivedi, R.S. (1997). The Emerging HRM Practices in India: The HRM Challenges. Managing Human Resources: Personnel Management in Indian Enterprise. New Delhi: Galgotia Publishing Company.

Engineer Arun M. (1999). Liberalization and Human Resource Management: Challenges for the Corporations of Tomorrow. Indian Journal of Industrial Relations, Vol. 35, No 1, July 1999, pp.131-133.

Gangee, Z; and Sengupta, U. (1999). In Human Company. Business World Case Studies, Apr-May 1999, p. 34-41.

Gani A. Ahad M. Osman (1996). International Transfer Of Management Technology And The Role of HRD: A Conceptual Model of the Transfer Process, November, www.nbs@ntv.edu.sg

Gary Dessler (1997). Tomorrow's HR Today: New Management Practices, Human Resource Management 7th Edition, p.13-15.

George Kuriyan (1999-2000). Changing Concept in Corporate Government and HRM Out Look For New Millennium.

Personal Today, Vol. 28, (1999-2000), p. 17. Calcutta: National Institute Of Personnel Management.

Gregory Shea, and Berg David. (1987). Analyzing The Development of An OD Practitioner, 1987, Journal of Applied Behavioural Science, Vol. 23 (3), 315-336.

Hackett, Thomas J, 1988 The Real Role Of Personnel Managers, 1988 (March), Personnel Journal, Vol. 67 (3), 70-75.

Hargreaves P and Jarvis P. (1997). The Human Resource Development Handbook (Rev. 2000 Ed.) London: Kogan Page Ltd. p. 80.

Hord L.Byars and Hestile W. Rue. (1987) Human Resource Management. Illinois: Irwine, Homelood. Second Ed.

Huselid, Mark A, (1995). The Impact of Human Resource Management Practices on Turnover, Productivity and Corporate Financial Performance, Academy of Management Journal, 1995 June, Vol. 38 (3), 635-672

Jain V.K. (1996) HRD Practices in Indian Industries, New Delhi: Anmol Publications Pvt. Ltd. pp. 36-61.

Jayaraman K. (1996). Personnel Managers Attitude towards Their Profession, Indian Journal of Applied Psychology, Vol. 33, No 1, 22-27.

Jean Woodall and Diana Winstanley (2000). Handbook of Management Development Strategizing and Practicing. New Delhi: Maya Publication Pvt. Ltd.

John M. Ivancevich (2001). Causes of Work Related Accidents and Illness, Human Resource Management. 8th Edition.

Hersey and Blanchard 2001 Management of Organization Behaviour. New Delhi: Prentice Hall of India Pvt. Ltd. (7th Ed) pp. 95-98.

http://www.dairy.com.au/careers/index.html

http://www.dairy.com.au/careers/index.html

http://humanresources.about.com/library/weekly/aa061100a.htm

http://humanresources.about.com/library/weekly/aa061100a.htm

http://academic.emporia.edu/smithwil/001fmg444pa/eja/webb.htm#Competitive

http://academic.emporia.edu/smithwil/001fmg444pa/eja/webb.htm#Competitive

Huselid, Mark A, (1995). The Impact of Human Resource Management Practices on Turnover, Productivity and Corporate Financial Performance, Academy Of Management Journal, 1995 June, Vol. 38 (3), 635-672

Indian Journal of Industrial Relations (1994) 'Emerging Trends in Industrial Relations and Human Resource Management In Indian Industry,' July 1994, Vol. 30, No 1, p. 19.

Indian Journal Of Industrial Relations 'Human Resources Management for the India Tomorrow,' October 1993, Vol. 29, No 2.Indian Journal of Industrial Relations (1994a). 'Human Resource Management Practices in India: An Exploratory Study', October 1994, Vol. 30, No 2, p.190.

Ivanwich John M and Michael T Matteson (1980). Stress at Work, Scotts: Foresman, Glenview, p. 5-9.

Jorsotia Punita (2002). HR Managers Gear Up to Combat New Challenges. www.promentor.fi/cca/HRmanagers.html www.itpeopleindia.com/20020121

Joseph, Jerome and Singh Kuldeep (1998). Organization Effectiveness through HRD. New Delhi: Oxford and IBH Publishing Co. Pvt. Ltd. pp. 1-6.

Kaila H.L. (1999). Attitudes and Perceptions of Female Executives towards Various Issues - A Psychological Analysis. Journal of Community Guidance and Research, 1999, Vol. 16. Issue 16, No. 2, pp. 121-139.

Kaila H. L. (2003). How Do Metro Managers Cope With Their Stresses, And Health Problems? The Journal of Health Management, 5,1, 2003, 139-144.

Kaila H.L. (2003). Organizational Behaviour & HRM', New Delhi: AITBS Publishers.

Kamoche Ken and Mueller Frank, (1998). Human Resource Management and The Appropriation – Learning Perspective, Human Relations, August 1998, Vol. 51 (8), 1033-1060.

Khandewak Preetam (1986). Perceived Need Satisfaction and Importance among Supervisory and Managerial Personnel, 1986, Indian Journal of Applied Psychology, Vol. 23 (I), p. 17-24.

Konrad, Alison M, Linehan, Frank (1995). Formalized HRM Structures: Co-ordinating Equal Employment Opportunity or Concealing Organizational Practices, Academy of Management Journal, June 1995, Vol. 38 (3), 787-820.

Koontz Harold and WeiHRich Heinz (1998). Essentials of Management. New Delhi: Tata McGraw-Hill 5th Edition. pp. 63-68.

Krishnan, R. (2002). The Hidden Battleground. The Smart Manager; vol. 1(2) p. 135-146

Laabs Jennifer J. (1996). HR Pioneers Explore the Road less Traveled, Personnel Journal, Vol. 75 (Feb-Dec 1996) p. 70.

Louellen Essex and Mitchell Kusy (2000). Fast Forward Leadership. New Delhi: Prentice Hall.

Malmgren, J.K. (2001). http://www.employmentinvancouver.com/index.html, http://www.employmentinvancouver.com/index.html

Mamoria C. B. (1996). Personnel Management (management of human resource). Mumbai, Himalaya Publishing House, pp. 54, 56.

Mathews Audrey (1998). Diversity: A Principle of Human Resource Management, Public Personnel Management, California State University, 1998, (Sum), Vol. 27(2), 175-185.

Mathew M.K. (1992). Managerial Satisfaction In Relation To On the Job-Activities. Psychological Studies, Vol. 37 (2 And 3), (University of Calicut) pp. 99-105.

Mathew M.K. (1989). Development of a Managerial Activity Scale, Psychological Studies, Vol. 34, No 2, p. 111-118.

Michael Hess, (1995). Development, Administration, Human Resources and Public Sector Reform, April 1995, Indian Journal of Industrial Relations, Vol. 30, No 4.

Michael, V. P. (1999). HR Manager and HR Management Process. Mumbai: Himalaya Publishing House, 5th Revised Ed.

M. N. Mishra and O. P. Rai (1999). Managerial Excellence. Jaipur: R.B.S.A Publications.

Monappa Arun and Mahrukh Engineer (2000). Liberalization and HRM – Challenges For Corporations of Tomorrow, New Delhi: Response Books Publications, pp. 85-86, 97-99.

Muchinsky P. M., (1998). Psychology Applied to Work. Wadsworth: Thompson Learning. Sixth edition.

Nair N.G and Latha Nair, (1999). Personnel Management and Industrial Relations. New Delhi: S. Chand and Company Ltd.

Newell, H. and Scarbrough, H (Ed.) (2002). Human Resource Management. New Delhi: Palgrave Publishers.

Paul Toulson and Philip Dewe, (1999). HR: Value or Expense? New Delhi: Tata McGraw Hill Publishing Company Ltd.

Panchanatham N. and Karuppiah K. R. K. (1993). A Study of Executive Leadership Styles and Problem Solving Behaviour, July 1993, Indian Journal of Industrial Relations, Vol. 29, No 1, pp.101-107.

Peter Sheal (1999). Importance of HR Managers and Supervisors in Staff Development, New Delhi: Crest Publishing House.

Prasad Kesho, (2000). Getting the Right People. New Delhi: Macmillan India Ltd.

Ramaswamy E.A. (2000). Managing Human Resources, A Contemporary Text. New Delhi: Oxford University Press.

Rao A.K. (1998-99). HR Challenges In the Coming Decades, Personnel Today, Vol. 19, p. 41. Calcutta: National Institute Of Personnel Management.

Rao P. Subba (2000). Qualifications and Qualities of HR Manager, Personnel and HRM Text and Cases. Mumbai: Himalaya Publishing House.

Rao P. Subba (2000). Role of HR Manager as A Specialist, Mumbai: Himalaya Publishing House.

Rao P. Subba (2000). Personnel and Human Resource Management, Millennium Edition Mumbai: Himalaya Publishing House.

Rao, T.V. (1990) Qualities and Competency Requirements of HRD Managers. New Delhi: Oxford and IBH Publishing Co. Pvt. Ltd.

Ratnam C, and Srivastava B. (1987). Personnel Management and Human Resources, ILO, World Labour Report, Vol. 2, (Ch. 9: Safety and Health), Geneva: McGraw Hill.

Reddy V.R.F., (1990). Strategic Environment and Implications for HRM, National Institute of Personnel Management, Calcutta: Willey Eastern Ltd.

Richman L.S. 1983, Health Benefits come Under the Knife. Fortune, May 2, p. 95-96.

Robbins S.P. (2000). Organizational Behaviour. New Delhi: Prentice Hall of India Pvt. Ltd. Eastern Economy Edition.

Robbins Stephen (2000). HR Managers – Essentials of Organizational Behaviour: (5th Edition) New Delhi: Prentice Hall of India Pvt. Ltd. pp. 66-75.

Rosemary Thomson and Christopher Mabey (1994). Developing human resources. Oxford: Butterworth-Heinmann Ltd.

Sastry M.B.S. (1999). HRD in the New Millennium. New Delhi: Tata McGraw Hill.

Satish Pai, S Ravishankar et al, (1999). Human Resource Development Skills for Organizational Excellence. Mumbai: Himalaya Publishing House.

Saxena Pradeep (2002). Back Injuries. Times of India (Ascent), Monday, October 21, 2002.

Sharma, A.M (1994). Personnel and Human Resource Management, Mumbai: Himalaya Publishing House, Page 255-258.

Silvera, D.M. (1990). Human Resource Development: The Indian Experience. (2nd Ed) New Delhi: News India Publications

Singh H.K. and Singh. Meera (1998). Frontiers of General Management. New Delhi: Kanishka Publishers.

Shiva Ramu S. (2000). 20th Century Management Tools and Techniques. New Delhi: A. H Wheeler Publishing.

Singh Shailendra (1989). Profiles of Stress Experiences: Variations across Ownership and Management Levels, April 1989, Indian Journal of Industrial Relations, Vol. 24, No 4, pp. 385-393.

Snell, Scott A, and Voundt, Mark A, (1995). Human Resource Management and Firm Performance: Testing A Contingency Model of Executive Controls, Journal Of Management, 1995, Vol. 21 (4), 711-737.

Sorab Sadri and Pranabesh Ray (1993). Human Resources Management For The India Of Tomorrow, Indian Journal of Industrial Relations, Vol. 29, No 2, Oct-1993, pp.157-167.

Sparks Kate and Cary L. Coopers (1999). Occupational Differences In the Work-Strain Relationship: Towards the Use of Situational Specific Models. Journal of Occupational and Organizational Psychology. Vol. 71, 1999, 219.

Srivastava K. B.L. (2000). Rethinking HR: Role Of HR Professionals In A Changing Business Environment, Indian Journal Of Industrial Relations, Vol. 35, No 4, April 2000, pp. 532-543.

Stranks J, (1997) A Manager's Guide To Health And Safety At Work. In: Hargreaves P. and Jarvis P. (1997). The Human Resource Development Handbook (Rev. 2000 Ed.) London: Kogan Page Ltd. p. 21. (5th Ed).

Subramani P.N. And G. Rajindra (2001). Human Resource Management and Industrial Relations. Mumbai: Himalaya Publishing House, (1st Ed).

Susan M. Heathfield (2001). http://www.http: // humanresources.about.com/mbody.htm and http:// humanresources.about.com/mbody.htm

Swanson V., Judith P. Walker and R.J. Simpson (2000). Psychological Job Strain and Productivity in Human Service

Workers: A Test of Demand-Control Support Model. Journal of Occupational and Organizational Psychology. Vol. 73, (2000) p. 501.

Thomson, R. and Mabey, C. (1994). Developing Human Resources. London: Butterworth and Heinemann.

William J. Rothwell, Robert K. Prescott, and Maria W. Taylor (1999). Strategic HR Leader, Mumbai: Jaico Publishing House.

www.aviationcareer.net/HR

www.gov.sg/mom/gen/mpn/000/index

www.HR_esource.com

www.odnetwork.org/odponline

www.WetFeet.com

Index

A

Abstract Conceptualization (AC), 119
Active Experimentation (AE), 119
Acquisition (role of HR in), 25
Aim of managers, 29
Alcoholism and drug abuse, 47
Appropriation of HRM, 62
Attitudes of employees, 94
Attributes (personal) of HR Managers, 73, 85-88

B

Bank Women Managers, 182
BCHRMA professional designation of HR Professional, 21
BCIT HRM Programme, 22
Behavioural disposition pattern, 111

C

CEO's (study on), 115
Challenges of
- HR Managers 30, 49, 147, 163-64
- coping with, 148

Challenges in future HRD, 99
Change process (necessity of), 65
Changing business environment and HR Professionals, 68, 76
Changes in HR work ways, 69
Change (managing) and HR Professionals, 75
Changing Concept in HRM, 101
Charismatic CEO's 115
CHRP (certified HR professional) designation, 21
Competitive advantage of company and HR, 33, 54
Competency types in HR, 90
Communication Skills HR manager, 34-35
- do's and don'ts, 35
- guidelines, 37

Concrete Experience (CE), 118 in managers, 121
Coping Skills of HR Managers, 160
Corporate Culture (old & new) and HR dept, 19
Cosmetic Executive women, 54
Coordination, 93

D

Decentralization, 32
Decision making, 105

Deloitte and Touche Survey, 52
- findings, 53

Dissonance (managing), 94
Diversity initiatives and HRM, 62
Downsizing decisions by HR managers, 21

E

E business women, 182
Emerging function of HR Managers, 158
Employees (accident prone), 43
Empowerment of employees, 33
Equal employment opportunity
- HRM practices in, 60

Exogeneous/Endogeneous variables of HRM functions, 71
Expectations from HR managers, 88

F

Farley Frank research of personality types, 116
Female Executive – Psychological Profile, 106
First Line Manager role, functions, 171
Functions of
- HRM, 167
- HR professionals, 154
- managers, 92, 158, 167

G

Gentech and HCC acquisition and HR role, 25-26
Gender and organizational level impact on leadership, 114
Getting the Right People, 65
Globalization/liberalization, 49
- challenges, 31

H

Health
- maintenance managers, 11
- of managers, 129

Health problems
- of HR managers, 134-35, 159, 169
- of women Managers, 180

Healthy and Safety
- program-factors effecting, 46
- of employees, 51
- work-guide to managers, 66

Hiring and firing of CEO's (study on), 115
HPWP (High Performance Work Practices), 61
HR Activities, 144
HRD
- meaning, 143
- strategies, 25
- applications, 25
- function-scenario in companies, 141
- missionary (attributes of), 80

HRD Systems and practices areas (Pareek and Rao), 98
HR Executive
- nature of work, 142, 144
- challenges, 143, 149

HR Leaders World Meet, 100
HRM
- for tomorrow, 63, 70
- practices, 64
- strategies, 38, 76-77
- emerging practices, 45
- goals, 45
- applications, 91
- primary goal, 58
- and turnover, 61

HR Managers
- areas, 96
- nature of job, 144-47
- attributes, 79, 85
- challenges, 147
- functions, 84
- and firms performance, 61
- expectations from, 88
- role, 55-56, 58
- qualities, 50

HR Professionals new role/goals, 9, 17-18
HR Successful attributes, 40
HR in India (Characteristics), 47
HR Strategy, 69
Human Resource
- and public sector reform, 64
- definition, 172

Human Factor in organization, 161
Human Quality Development (HQD), 41

I

Ideological Influences HRM, 71
Important Area of HR Managers Involvement, 96
India
- HR profesion in, 72
- HR practices in, 98

Individual HR Managers
- stresses, 132
- health problems, 135-136
- perception of HRD, 150-152

Industrialization impact of, 32
Insights of some HR Managers, 162
International HRM, 104
Integrated HRD Approach, 82
IT implementation resistance, 24

J

Job Strain levels, 101
Job Stress and Burnout, 47
Job satisfaction, 105
Just in Time (JIT), 39

K

Kolb's Experimental Learning Theory, 112

L

Language use/fluency of managers, 29
Larsen & Toubro and HRD, 174
Leadership, 105
- styles, 72, 113
- meaning, 118
- ability of managers, 28

Learning
- meaning, 118
- styles of managers, 122
- on the job, 93
- styles (research on), 112

Legislations (labour) impact, 33

Liberalization and HRM, 67

M

Management
- development, 23
- tools and techniques, 22-23
- and HR, 166
- Technology and role of HRD, 83
- of organization behaviours, 94

Managing organizational change, 42
Managers/ supervisors role, 74
Managerial Psychology, 122
Managers
- personality types, 119
- leadership styles, 120-21
- learning styles, 121

Manpower Costs, 34
Mantras for 20th Century Management, 41
Mass Movement impact, 33
Mechanisms and Process Linkages in HRD, 99
Mentoring and Coaching, 104
Mumbai Managers Personality types, 123

N

National Commission on Labour (NCL) Report on HR, 47
- Characteristics, 47

Nature of work (HR Managers), 153
National Institute of Personnel Management (NIPM)
- survey on trends in personnel management, 77-79

National Centre for Vocational Education Research (NCVER), 112
New
- concept of management, 177
- roles of HR professionals, 9, 17-18
- management practices, 44

New HR
- professional, 157
- dept, 163

New Industrial Relations and HR Politics, 62

O

Occupations having work pressure, 102-103
Open style of management, 76
Organizational culture, 103
Organization development intervention, 105
Organizational effectiveness and HRD, 99
Organisational Behaviour Essentials, 93
Organizational Restruetur, 67
OSHA model of human behaviour, 41

P

Perception of
- HRD scenario by HR managers, executives, 149,

169
- Women managers, 184-90

Performance Appraisal, 104
Personnel Management Territory of , 32
Personnel Manager
- role, 56
- attitude towards their profession, 60
- and HRD manager integration, 84

Personality of managers, 109
Personality, 117
- type T, 110
- type A, 117
- type B, 117

Planning HR, 91
Public Sector Reform and HRM, 64

Q

Quality of Employees, 33
Quality of HR Manager, 10, 80
Quality of Work Life (QWL), 68
Qualifications of HR Manager, 73, 80-81

R

Recruitment and Selection, 91, 104
Recruitment Outsourcing, 25
Reflective Observations (RO), 119
- in managers, 122

Researches in
- HR–conclusions, 106
- Learning styles, 112-17

Reward Management, 91
Role of HR, 40
- professional, 20, 24, 70, 164
- work in future, 89

S

School Principle, 182
Scientific Management, 23
Social responsibility/ responsiveness of Managers, 34
Staff development, 75
Strategy (HR), 38,76
Strategic Planning and HRM, 91
Stress and HR, 51
Stress Management by HR Managers, 66
Stress and Health problems of Metro Managers, 97, 129
Stresses as HR Managers, 130, 154
- types, 131
- individual types, 132
- coping with, 136-37
- styles, 138-40

Stresses of Women Managers, 179

T

Technical Change in the Organization, 23
Technical Competence needed by a Manager, 26
Technological Change
- challenges of, 27

Technical Competence, 28
Top Managers Role, 30
Total Quality Management

(TQM), 39
- features, 39

Training of effectiveness, 106
Type
- A personality
- B personality
- T personality

Transactional/Transformational leadership, 113, 118

W

Women Managers, 104, 177
- in HR (perceptions of) 170-71
- issues concerning, 178
- stresses, 179
- health problems, 180
- coping with challenges, 180-81
- message to, 183
- action plan, 190

Women entrepreneurs, 54
Work place injuries, 52
Work pressure
- sources of, 102
- occupations, 102

Work Related Accidents and Illness, 43
- Causes, 43